Sheet
Pan
Sweets

Sheet Pan Sweets

SIMPLE, STREAMLINED DESSERT RECIPES

MOLLY GILBERT

Photographs by Dana Gallagher

**UNION
SQUARE
& CO.**

NEW YORK

ISBN 978-1-4549-4666-3
ISBN 978-1-4549-4667-0 (e-book)

For information about custom editions, special sales, and premium purchases, please contact specialsales@unionsquareandco.com.

Printed in Canada

2 4 6 8 10 9 7 5 3 1

unionsquareandco.com

Interior design by Raphael Geroni

For Calder, Jack, and Sadie, my sweetest companions,
both in the kitchen and out

Contents

PIES & THE LIKE

BREAKFAST & BREADS

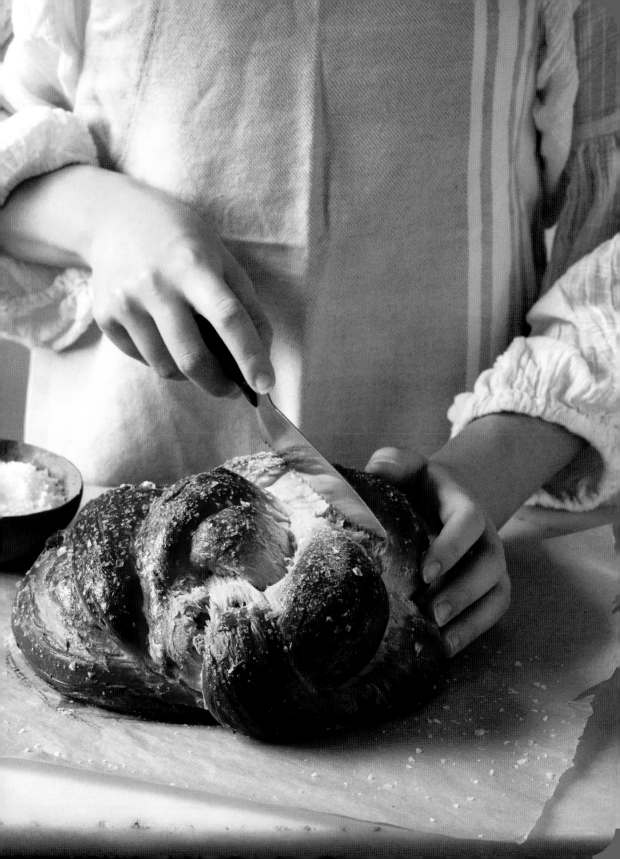

Introduction

When I wrote my first cookbook, *Sheet Pan Suppers*, nearly ten years ago, I had no idea that sheet pan cooking, as both a concept and a food trend, would skyrocket to popularity. Today, sheet pan recipes flood the internet, and cookbooks dedicated to sheet pan cooking are seemingly everywhere. It's nothing really new, of course—sheet pans have been around for decades and restaurant cooks have been using them for just as long—but for the home cook (or the busy parent, the hungry student, the host and hostess intent on feeding a crowd), the ease, simplicity, and elegance of cooking a whole meal on one sheet pan has been a game changer. I'm so glad to have any part in this "trend" and that it seems here to stay.

The really good news for us, though (and by "us" I mean we of the sweet teeth—you wouldn't be here if you didn't feel incomplete without dessert at pretty much every meal, would you?), is that sheet pan *baking* is just as wonderful and game changing as its savory counterpart. It's true! I graduated from culinary and pastry school over a decade ago, and I've been happily baking away, both professionally and personally, ever since. This book is my opportunity to address the center of the Venn diagram of my areas of expertise—sheet pans and baking—and I really couldn't be more delighted. Here's what I know: the joys of sheet pan baking are threefold—volume, quick bake times, and quick cooling.

What do I mean by "volume"? Well, you can make *a lot* of dessert on one sheet pan. Need to crank out a boatload of treats for the school bake sale? Or maybe you're hosting a massive Friendsgiving feast? I've got you! (I highly recommend going with Buckeye Bars, page 116, for the former and Pumpkin Pie Bars, page 111, for the latter.) The massive surface area of the humble half sheet ensures that there will be cake, bars, cookies, slab pie, and more to feed a crowd.

Quick bake times and quick cooling pretty much speak for themselves, and I've got science to back me up here—the large surface area and shallow sides of a sheet pan help cakes bake up more quickly than they would in more traditional round, square, or rectangular cake, loaf, or Bundt pans, and they'll cool in a fraction of the time it would take those other pans, too, which ultimately means you'll have cake in your face (not still in your pan) like, now. Have I sold you yet?

You'll find this book divided up into six delicious chapters: Sheet Cakes, Layered & Rolled Cakes, Cookies, Bars, Pies & the Like, and Breakfast & Breads. My goal in each chapter is to give you simple, sweet, streamlined recipes to help you fill that block party table, light up that holiday cookie swap, and fulfill that birthday wish. Because no meal is complete without dessert. So what are we waiting for? Let's give sheet pan baking a whirl!

Tools & Equipment

A Sheet Pan Primer

A quick word on equipment and ingredients! Let's get our ducks in a row. First and foremost, let's talk sheet pans.

For the recipes in this book, I use a half sheet pan, also called a rimmed baking sheet, which is a flat, rectangular metal pan that measures 18 × 13 inches and has a 1-inch rim around the sides. Sheet pans are usually made out of aluminum or stainless steel, and these days many varieties come with a nonstick coating. In general, I prefer the plain aluminum or stainless-steel varieties, although for baking, the nonstick layer can be useful; either variety will work for the recipes in this book.

It's important to note that a jelly-roll pan, which has the same shape as a sheet pan, is *not* sheet pan equivalent—jelly-roll pans are smaller and less sturdy than true sheet pans, and they will not work for the recipes here. You'll get a lot of overflow and oven spillage, which, trust me, you'd rather avoid. So, sorry to be exclusive, but only sheet pans are invited to this particular party.

If you're into the quick cooking and cooling benefits of sheet pan baking but have less need for volume, you may want to invest in a quarter sheet pan. These are tiny sheet pans—at 13 × 9 inches, they're half the size of a regular half sheet pan and work well if you want to bake just half a recipe (or if your oven is adorably, comically small, like the one in my beloved fourth-floor walk-up apartment in San Francisco many years ago).

Everything Else

Now that we've got the all-important pan figured out, what else will we need? Just a few other items. Here's what I like to keep on hand for sheet pan baking:

Parchment paper and nonstick baking spray: To make sure our perfect bakes don't get stuck! For baking spray, I like to use regular-old PAM, though any kind of neutral oil spray will do the trick. I buy parchment paper in a big box of precut sheets, which I find saves a lot of time and hassle, as they conform perfectly to the size and shape of my sheet pans.

Nesting bowls for mixing: You don't need many, but one good large bowl and a few smaller ones are a must for most of the recipes in this book. I have sets of both stainless-steel and glass mixing bowls, and I find I reach for the stainless-steel ones the most, as they're sturdy yet light. Glass bowls are great when I need a microwave-safe option.

Balloon whisk: I use my trusty 10-inch balloon whisk for everything from mixing up dry ingredients to aerating simple cake batters to drizzling glaze over a finished cake or bar recipe. Smaller ones are cute and fun, but the 10-incher is your kitchen workhorse.

Stand mixer or handheld electric mixer: Although many of the recipes in this book can be made without a mixer, some can't be (unless you have superhuman strength and enjoy making buttercream or meringue by hand—and if that's the case, I tip my hat to you and your Michael B. Jordan muscles). I've had and loved my KitchenAid stand mixer for years. When I started baking more with my young kids, I found having a smaller handheld option useful and easy for their little hands to maneuver. Neither needs to be fancy.

Measuring tools: I love my simple, stainless-steel measuring cups (my set has sizes from ¼ cup to 1 cup) for dry (sugars, flours, etc.) or semi-solid (sour cream, pumpkin puree, jam, nut butters) ingredients. When I measure my dry ingredients, I use the scoop-and-sweep method: I mix up my flour to aerate it, scoop my measuring cup full, then sweep excess flour from the top with a knife to level it. I find the scoop-and-sweep (not to be confused with the bend-and-snap) less fiddly and time consuming than other methods. I also have a few different-size spouted glass and plastic measuring cups for liquids (water, juice, milk, oil). To ensure accuracy, it's important to use the dry cups for dry ingredients, and the spouted measuring cups for liquids. A good set of standard measuring spoons, in increments from ⅛ teaspoon to 1 tablespoon, is vital for measuring ingredients like baking soda, baking powder, and spices.

Rubber spatula: A good, flexible rubber spatula will pay dividends in smooth, well-mixed batters and cleanly scraped mixing bowls. I have a set from Williams-Sonoma that's lasted me years.

Offset spatula: A true kitchen gem! I have two sizes—large (7½ inches) and small (4½ inches)—and use both with enthusiastic regularity. Everything from spreading batter in a pan, transferring baked cookies to a wire cooling rack, and swooping frosting or glaze over a finished bake is made easier with an offset spatula by your side. I like the ones made by Ateco.

Microplane zester: A Microplane is useful for more than just citrus zest (though it is indeed excellent for that, and I do encourage a lot of lemon, lime, and orange zesting in the recipes here). I also use it to grate nutmeg and finely shave chocolate bars.

Cookie scoops: The absolute easiest way to ensure round and uniform cookies! I have a few different sizes, though I reach most often for my 1½- and 2-tablespoon-size scoops. My favorite versions are made by OXO.

Paring knife: The smallest knife in the arsenal, a simple paring knife helps to loosen sticky cakes from the pan before turning them out and/or slicing them. Your paring knife doesn't need to be fancy; it just should feel good in your hand and have a reliably sharp blade.

Food processor or blender: Although not needed for most recipes, I use my trusty old (really old! These things last forever) Cuisinart food processor to occasionally pulse together a quick pie dough, grind up toasted nuts, or whip up a batch of frangipane or even buttercream.

Fine-mesh sieve: I find having one large and one small sieve to be very useful in baking—the large one is great for sifting together dry ingredients to ensure your batters remain lump-free, and the small one helps gracefully dust the tops of cakes and treats with a snowfall of confectioners' sugar or cocoa powder.

Rolling pin: For when we need a perfect piecrust! I like French-style wooden rolling pins with tapered edges, but any kind will work, so long as it feels comfortable in your hands.

Wire cooling rack: Having at least one good large wire cooling rack is immensely helpful for sheet pan baking. You can use smaller ones, but you run the risk of your pans wobbling or, worse, toppling while setting up to cool. So if you can, when it comes to the cooling rack, go big.

Oven thermometer: Having a small metal oven thermometer perched inside your oven will help ensure that your oven temperature is correct and consistent. All ovens are different, depending on make, model, vintage, calibration, and general quirkiness (a truly real thing), and it's important to get to know yours to ensure your bakes come out the way you want them to. Does your oven have hot spots? Does it take a really long time to preheat? A sturdy oven thermometer is the only way to find out and course correct.

Ingredients

What about ingredients? These are the ones I keep stocked in my fridge and pantry so I can bake up something delicious whenever the craving strikes.

Flour: I always have all-purpose flour on hand (I like using unbleached varieties, and King Arthur is my favorite brand), and since it's the most widely available variety, all-purpose is the kind of flour used most often here. Occasionally, you'll find a recipe that calls for cake flour or another special variety like buckwheat, almond, or oat flour. I'll only recommend these when I think it makes a real difference in the taste or texture of the final product—and in a pinch, you can usually just use all-purpose flour instead.

Salt: I'm often asked if salt is really necessary in sweet treats—the answer is a resounding yes! Salt enhances the flavor of everything it touches, and it's especially important for balancing out the sweetness of baked goods. I cook and bake exclusively with Diamond Crystal kosher salt, which is flakier and less dense than plain table salt or fine sea salt. It has a fresh, clean flavor and tastes less salty by volume than other varieties (including Morton's kosher salt). If you're using a different brand or type of salt, be sure to use less than the amount called for so your bakes don't taste too salty. The only other kind of salt used in these recipes is flaky sea salt, such as Maldon, for finishing. Just a sprinkle can really take a cookie or bar recipe over the top flavorwise, so don't skimp!

Eggs: I always use large eggs for baking—any color or grade will do, so long as they're large. Often eggs will incorporate more smoothly into batters and doughs if they're used at room temperature, but these recipes are pretty forgiving; if you forgot to or don't have time to let your eggs warm up, feel free to use them cold, straight from the fridge.

Unsalted butter: Emphasis on *unsalted*! Unsalted butter is fresher than salted, and it's best for baking. Our butter doesn't control the amount of salt we're adding to our recipes—we do, okay?

Sugars: I use four kinds of sugar with regularity—granulated white sugar, brown sugar (light and dark will work interchangeably in the recipes here, unless I've called for one or the other specifically), confectioners' sugar (for sweetening whipped cream, keeping rolled cakes from sticking, and decorative dusting), and coarse raw sugar like turbinado or demerara for texture and crunch.

Milk and dairy: I always use whole-milk or full-fat dairy in my recipes. Milk, sour cream, yogurt, cream cheese, and heavy cream are at their best, flavor- and texture-wise, when they've got that fat, but if all you have is 2%, that'll do. I occasionally call for buttermilk, which is lovely for a bit of tang and lift in recipes, but if you don't have any on hand it's simple to stir together a substitute: Mix 1 tablespoon lemon juice or white vinegar per every 1 cup milk you need, give it a stir, and let it sit for 10 minutes. Voilà! Buttermilk.

Extracts: I'm a big believer in pure vanilla extract, and I use it with abandon. I like to make my own by stuffing a jar with whole vanilla beans (beanilla.com has a good variety), then pouring in vodka or bourbon to cover. After a few short months of infusing in a dark cabinet at room temperature, you've got a big jar of homemade vanilla extract ready to roll!

Other extracts you'll find here are pure almond extract, coconut extract, and pure peppermint extract. I use these sparingly, as they pack quite a punch and can taste odd and fake if overused, but a little hit every now and again can help boost flavors and complete our bakes.

Chocolate: I keep so many different types of chocolate on hand that the basket in my pantry is nearly bursting. I like options! I enjoy collecting bars of good-quality bittersweet and milk chocolate for both snacking and chopping into cookies or melting for ganache, and bags on bags of bittersweet, semisweet, milk, and white chocolate chips and chunks for every cookie, cake, and bar baking need. My favorite chip brands are Ghirardelli and Guittard.

Cocoa powder: A real powerhouse in packing in that chocolate flavor punch. It's important to use the best unsweetened cocoa powder you can find. I like to use Dutch-process cocoa, which is less acidic and has a darker color and smoother flavor than natural cocoa (I find the Droste brand at my local supermarket), but for most of the recipes in this book, unless otherwise noted, you can use either natural or Dutch-process cocoa with success.

Oils: Any kind of neutral (aka flavorless) oil will work in the cakes, cookies, doughs, and treats found here; I usually call for pure vegetable or canola oil, but you can easily substitute safflower, corn, or grapeseed oil without incident. When olive oil is called for, look for a light, fruity variety.

Spices: A well-stocked spice rack can really make your baked goods sing—make sure you replace your spices every six months or so to keep them fresh and flavorful. If you'd rather not commit to a whole jar, check the bulk bins at your local store, where you can buy smaller amounts to fit your needs. The spices I reach for most in baking include ground cinnamon, ginger, cardamom, allspice, and cloves and whole nutmeg.

Poppy seeds, white or black sesame seeds, and a small jar of instant espresso powder round out my collection.

Freeze-dried fruit: I love using freeze-dried fruit in baking for its ability to bring big, concentrated fruit flavor without adding any extra moisture. I find bags of freeze-dried strawberries, raspberries, apples, and more at my local grocery store, usually in the dried fruit or snack food section.

Jams and sauces: I feel a little naked without jars of both apricot and raspberry jam in my kitchen at all times (Bonne Maman is my favorite brand). I like to collect other, more interesting flavors of jam and marmalade to raise the stakes in a classic Victoria sponge (page 68), for example, or to swirl into some whipped cream for an all-star cake filling or meringue topper. Processed peanut butter is a must for baking (Skippy girl, here), and having a well-mixed jar of tahini on hand doesn't hurt, either. I also keep small jars of good-quality store-bought caramel for days when I just need a quick drizzle (maybe for the Salty Sweet Brown Sugar Cookie Bars, page 100?). I guess I'm just a jammy, saucy kind of gal, and I make no apologies for that.

Substitutions

I get it—people like to make recipe substitutions. Maybe you don't have an ingredient that's called for, or maybe you're just one of those people who likes to do things their own way. If you don't make the recipe as written, I can't guarantee success, since each recipe has been tested with the specific ingredients and amounts listed, but you know what? It's fine! Go wild! But, like, just a little bit wild. We can (usually) make it work. Here are some classic time-tested ingredient substitutions that work in a pinch.

Buttermilk: If you're out of buttermilk, you can use the vinegar/lemon juice and regular milk trick I mentioned earlier (see page 17), or you can thin out sour cream or yogurt with water or milk until it reaches the consistency of heavy cream.

Sour cream: Plain Greek yogurt can be happily substituted for sour cream. Vice versa, too.

Brown sugar: Out of brown sugar? Make your own by combining 1 cup granulated sugar with 1 tablespoon unsulfured molasses (not blackstrap) and mixing like the dickens until uniformly brown.

Confectioners' sugar: Also called powdered sugar! If you're staring at the bottom of the bag of confectioners' sugar, simply make your own by blitzing together 1 cup granulated sugar and 1 tablespoon cornstarch in a food processor or high-speed blender until soft and downy.

Nuts: Different kinds of nuts can often be swapped in a recipe without incident—if you don't like pecans, go ahead and use walnuts. Not a fan of almonds? Try peanuts or pistachios instead. Just keep general shape and size in mind.

Fruit: Fruit substitutions can be tricky, since different fruits have different flavors and water content, but the general rule is that fruits in the same family can usually be substituted in baking. That means pears for apples, nectarines or plums for peaches, and raspberries or blueberries for blackberries are all safe bets.

If you're **vegan or gluten-free** and are looking to adapt the recipes in this book, I've had good luck using Bob's Red Mill gluten-free flour blend (the one in the blue bag), which can be substituted one-for-one with regular all-purpose flour. As for flax eggs and aquafaba and butter substitutes, well, I can't vouch for those. You'll find a bunch of naturally gluten-free recipes here, though, so if that's your focus, I invite you to check out the recipes for Kitchen Sink Cookies (page 134), Flourless Peanut Butter Oaties (page 138), Blackberry Coconut Macaroons (page 149), Orange & Cream Mini Pavlovas (page 171), Butter Mochi Squares (page 112), Mint Chocolate Chip Meringue Roll (page 81), and Eton's Largest Mess (page 186).

So, we've got all our equipment, ingredients, and acceptable substitutions down, have we? Fire up the oven! Whisks in formation! Let's get this sheet (pan) started.

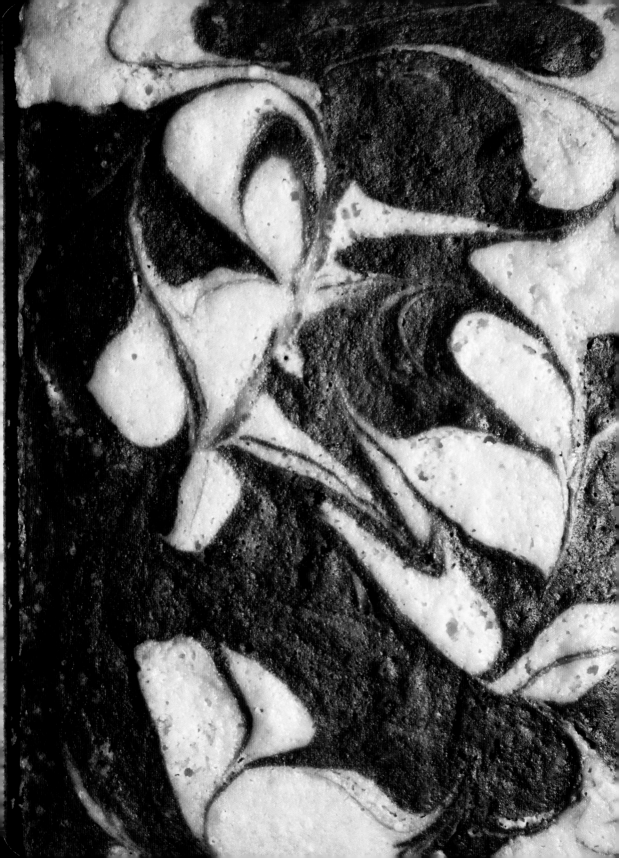

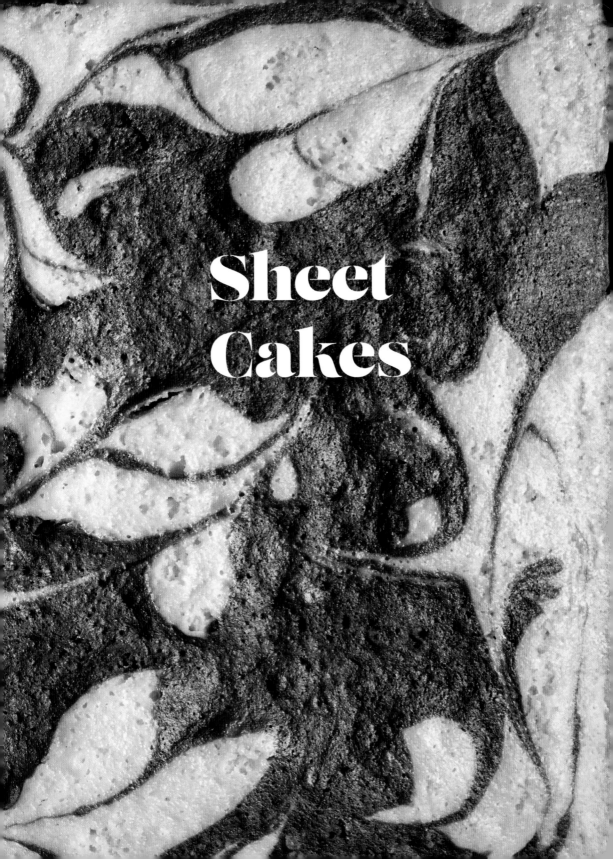

Sheet
Cakes

The Classic

What is it about sheet cake that's just so dang perfect? Is it the sweet, single-layer, served-straight-from-the-pan simplicity? The ease of assembly? The large canvas for decoration? Yes, yes, and yes. But I think the perfection of the sheet cake lies in its pure, sugary sense of nostalgia. When I think of sheet cakes, I think of my sunny, chaotic sixth birthday party in my parents' backyard, where we decorated little boxes with giant plastic jewels and had both egg races and a few close calls with the piñata stick (we were just really excited for that candy, you know?). I still remember the colorful swoops of icing on my birthday cake, and how I really, *really* wanted a piece with a pink flower.

You'll find plenty of opportunities for nostalgia in this chapter, from Jack's Chocolate Chip Cake with Fudge Frosting (page 26) to a Giant Flag Cake (page 43) and a classic Double Chocolate Sheet Cake (page 48), but you'll also find some fun twists on the theme, like Triple Citrus Poke Cake (page 36), Coconut Tres Leches (page 33), and a gooey, scoopable German's Chocolate Crater Cake (page 39). Serve them with or without a piñata—just know that all the cakes in this chapter are designed to feed a crowd and make hearts happy.

Jack's Chocolate Chip Cake

with
Fudge Frosting

SERVES 24

This cake is the one my younger son, Jack, asked for on his third birthday—and let me tell you: The child's got taste. I mean, he also asked for a garbage truck, but this cake! It's the perfect combination of fluffy vanilla cake and thick chocolate frosting, studded throughout with mini chocolate chips for some added texture. The cake is a simple one-bowl affair, and the fudge frosting whips up quickly with the help of a food processor (though if you don't have one, you can whisk it up almost as quickly with a handheld mixer). Toy garbage truck decoration optional, but encouraged.

Cake

Nonstick cooking spray

6 large eggs, at room temperature

2½ cups granulated sugar

½ cup (1 stick) unsalted butter, melted and cooled

1 cup canola oil

2 cups buttermilk

1 tablespoon pure vanilla extract

¼ teaspoon pure almond extract

4 cups all-purpose flour

1 tablespoon baking powder

1 teaspoon baking soda

1 teaspoon kosher salt

2 cups mini chocolate chips

Frosting

6 ounces unsweetened chocolate, melted and cooled

4½ cups confectioners' sugar

1½ cups (3 sticks) unsalted butter, at room temperature

⅓ cup heavy cream or half-and-half

1 tablespoon pure vanilla extract

1. MAKE THE CAKE: Preheat the oven to 350°F with a rack in the center position. Grease a sheet pan with nonstick spray.

2. In a large bowl, vigorously whisk together the eggs and granulated sugar for 1 minute, until well combined and very frothy. Whisk in the melted butter, canola oil, buttermilk, vanilla, and almond extract until smooth.

3. Add the flour, baking powder, baking soda, and salt and gently fold with the whisk until the batter is smooth and streak-free. Fold in the chocolate chips with a rubber spatula.

4. Pour the batter into the prepared pan and spread it evenly to the corners with a large offset spatula. Bake for 18 to 20 minutes, until the cake is golden and pulls away from the sides of the pan and a tester inserted into the center comes out clean.

5. Run a paring knife around the edges of the cake to loosen, then let the cake cool completely in the pan, about 25 minutes.

6. MEANWHILE, MAKE THE FROSTING: In a food processor, combine the melted chocolate, confectioners' sugar, butter, cream, and vanilla and process until smooth and creamy. If the frosting seems too soft, let it firm up in the refrigerator for about 15 minutes, then give it one last buzz in the food processor before using it.

7. Swoop the frosting over the cake in a thick, even layer. Slice into pieces and serve. The cake will keep, tightly covered, in the refrigerator for up to a week.

Ben's Carrot-Zucchini Cake

with Cream Cheese Frosting

SERVES 24

My husband, Ben, a very sensible eater, enjoys the occasional sweet treat but doesn't have to have them daily (like I do), so it makes sense that his favorite cake is stuffed with not just one but two types of vegetables. Truth be told, the carrots and zucchini give this cake a wonderfully moist, delicate texture, and the warm spices and bright cream cheese frosting round out the whole thing beautifully. I like making this cake around Easter and decorating the top with pastel sprinkles and candy-coated chocolate eggs, but it's perfect even unadorned—and a welcome sight any time of year.

Cake

Nonstick cooking spray

2½ cups all-purpose flour

2 teaspoons baking powder

1 teaspoon baking soda

1 teaspoon ground cinnamon

½ teaspoon freshly grated nutmeg

1 teaspoon kosher salt

4 large eggs

1½ cups granulated sugar

½ cup packed brown sugar

1½ cups canola oil

1 teaspoon pure vanilla extract

1½ cups shredded carrots

1½ cups shredded zucchini

Frosting

2 (8-ounce) packages cream cheese, at room temperature

¾ cup (1½ sticks) unsalted butter, at room temperature

2½ cups confectioners' sugar

Zest of 1 lemon

2 tablespoons sour cream or plain full-fat Greek yogurt

1 tablespoon pure vanilla extract

Kosher salt

1. MAKE THE CAKE: Preheat the oven to 350°F with a rack in the center position. Grease a sheet pan with nonstick spray.

2. In a medium bowl, whisk together the flour, baking powder, baking soda, cinnamon, nutmeg, and salt.

3. In the bowl of a stand mixer fitted with the whisk attachment or in a large bowl with a handheld mixer, whip together the eggs, granulated sugar, and brown sugar on high speed until pale yellow and thick, about 5 minutes.

4. While still whipping, slowly drizzle in the oil. When the oil is fully incorporated, whip in the vanilla. Add the flour mixture and whisk on low speed just until a smooth batter comes together, about 30 seconds. Use a rubber spatula to fold in the carrots and zucchini.

5. Pour the batter into the prepared pan and spread it evenly to the corners with a large offset spatula. Bake for 15 to 20 minutes, until the sides pull away from the pan and the cake springs back when you gently poke it in the middle. Place the pan on a wire rack and let the cake cool completely, about 25 minutes.

6. MEANWHILE, MAKE THE FROSTING: In the bowl of a stand mixer fitted with the paddle attachment or in a large bowl with a handheld mixer, cream together the cream cheese and butter on medium-high speed until smooth, about 3 minutes. With the mixer running, slowly add the confectioners' sugar, and beat well until the frosting is light and fluffy, about 3 minutes. Beat in the lemon zest, sour cream, vanilla, and a pinch of salt until smooth.

7. Swoop the frosting on top of the cake in a thick, even layer. Slice into pieces and serve. The cake will keep, uncovered (or covered with plastic wrap once the frosting hardens a bit), in the refrigerator for up to 3 days.

Marbled Pound Cake

SERVES 24

I love the dense richness of pound cake, plus the fact that it's so adaptable to different flavor combinations. Classic vanilla is a keeper, and a deep chocolate version is a fun twist. But why choose between the two? We can make just one batter and have both—a whole sheet pan of both, actually. Capped with a light, orangey glaze, we're covering all our pound cake bases. (If you'd prefer a straight vanilla glaze here, simply omit the orange zest and use milk instead of orange juice.)

Cake

Nonstick cooking spray

3½ cups all-purpose flour

1 tablespoon baking powder

1 teaspoon kosher salt

6 tablespoons (¾ stick) unsalted butter, melted

⅓ cup unsweetened Dutch-process cocoa powder

¾ cup (1½ sticks) unsalted butter, at room temperature

3 cups granulated sugar

6 large eggs

1 tablespoon pure vanilla extract

Zest of 1 orange

1 cup sour cream

Glaze

1 cup confectioners' sugar

Zest of 1 orange

3 tablespoons fresh orange juice

1 tablespoon pure vanilla extract

1. MAKE THE CAKE: Preheat the oven to 350°F with a rack in the center position. Grease a sheet pan with nonstick spray.

2. In a large bowl, whisk together the flour, baking powder, and salt.

3. In a medium bowl, whisk together the melted butter and cocoa powder until smooth.

4. In the bowl of a stand mixer fitted with the paddle attachment or in a large bowl with a handheld mixer, beat together the room-temperature butter and granulated sugar on medium-high speed until well combined but still a bit sandy, about 3 minutes. Add the eggs one at a time, beating until smooth and scraping down the sides of the bowl after each addition. Add the vanilla, orange zest, and sour cream and beat on low speed to combine. Add the flour mixture and mix on low speed until the batter just comes together and no streaks of flour remain.

5. Scoop half the batter in random ¼-cup dollops all over the prepared pan, covering roughly half of it.

6. Add the cocoa powder mixture to the remaining batter in the bowl and use a rubber spatula to fold it in until smooth and combined.

7. Dollop the chocolate batter around the vanilla batter on the pan. Spread and swirl a knife or small offset spatula through the batter several times to push it to the edges of the pan and achieve a marbled look. Bake for 20 to 25 minutes, until the cake is golden and just pulling away from the edges of the pan and a tester inserted into the center comes out clean. Transfer to a wire rack and allow the cake to cool completely in the pan, about 25 minutes.

8. MAKE THE GLAZE: In a medium bowl, whisk together the confectioners' sugar, orange zest, orange juice, and vanilla until smooth. Spread the glaze over the cooled cake. Slice into pieces and serve. The cake will keep, tightly covered, at room temperature for up to a week.

Coconut Tres Leches Cake

SERVES 24

Typically a sponge cake soaked in three types of milk (evaporated, condensed, and whole) with Latin American roots, tres leches cake is one of my favorites. I love how it straddles the line between cake and pudding, the soft cake swathed in cool creaminess both atop and below. This version strays from authenticity with the addition of coconut—three forms of coconut, actually. We'll add some extract to the cake, swap in coconut milk for evaporated milk in the drizzle, and top the whole thing with some sweet toasted coconut shreds. Toasting coconut is easy on a sheet pan—simply spread it out in a single layer and bake it in a 350°F oven for 5 to 8 minutes, tossing occasionally, until golden brown and fragrant.

Cake

Nonstick cooking spray

1 cup (2 sticks) unsalted butter, at room temperature

1¾ cups sugar

5 large eggs

3 cups all-purpose flour

2½ teaspoons baking powder

½ teaspoon kosher salt

1¼ cups whole milk

¼ cup vegetable oil

1 tablespoon pure vanilla extract

1 teaspoon coconut extract

Drizzle

1 (14-ounce) can full-fat coconut milk

1 (14-ounce) can sweetened condensed milk

1 cup whole milk

Frosting

2 cups heavy cream, cold

¼ cup sugar

Zest of 1 lime

1 cup sweetened shredded coconut, toasted (see headnote)

1. MAKE THE CAKE: Preheat the oven to 350°F with a rack in the center position. Grease a sheet pan with nonstick spray.

2. In the bowl of a stand mixer fitted with the paddle attachment or in a large bowl with a handheld mixer, cream together the butter and sugar on medium-high speed until light and fluffy, 3 to 5 minutes. Add the eggs one at a time, beating well and scraping down the sides of the bowl after each addition (don't worry if the mixture starts to look curdled; it will come together as you add more ingredients).

3. In a large bowl, whisk together the flour, baking powder, and salt.

4. In a large, spouted measuring cup, whisk together the milk, oil, vanilla, and coconut extract.

5. Alternate adding the dry ingredients and the wet ingredients to the egg mixture, starting and ending with the dry ingredients and mixing on low speed after each addition, then mix just until a smooth batter comes together.

6. Pour the batter into the prepared pan and spread it evenly to the corners with a large offset spatula. Bake until the sides of the cake pull away from the pan and a tester inserted into the center comes out clean, 35 to 40 minutes.

7. MEANWHILE, MAKE THE DRIZZLE: In a medium bowl, whisk together the coconut milk, condensed milk, and whole milk.

8. Use a toothpick or skewer to poke holes all over the warm cake, then slowly pour the drizzle over the top. It's important to go slowly here to allow the cake to soak up the drizzle; it will seem like too much, but don't panic! Some will be absorbed, and some will create that delicious little lake at the bottom when you slice the cake. Allow the cake to cool completely, about 20 minutes.

recipe continues

9. MEANWHILE, MAKE THE FROSTING: In the bowl of a stand mixer fitted with the whisk attachment or in a large bowl with a hand-held mixer, whip together the cream and sugar until stiff peaks form, about 5 minutes. Gently fold in the lime zest with a rubber spatula.

10. Spread the frosting generously over the cake. Top with the toasted coconut. Serve immediately, or store, tightly covered, in the refrigerator for up to 3 days.

Tell Me: **Why Does My Heavy Cream Need to be Cold Before Whipping?**

Ever had cream that just wouldn't whip? Temperature may be to blame! Heavy cream needs to be cold from the fridge to whip up properly. Why? Because the fat in the cream solidifies when chilled, and those firm fat globules trap more air bubbles while whipping—ultimately producing the fluffiest whipped cream. Stay cool!

Chocolate Pear Cake

SERVES 24

Here fresh pears bring delicate flavor and moisture to an easy chocolate cake. Topped with a simple, lightly spiced pear glaze, a slice of this cake is a humble, unexpected joy. It's best to use firmer pears here, as they're easier to grate into the batter—I like Anjou or Bosc. If you have any trouble finding pear sauce for the glaze, applesauce substitutes seamlessly.

Cake

Nonstick cooking spray

2 large eggs

1 cup packed brown sugar

¾ cup granulated sugar

½ cup vegetable oil

½ cup (1 stick) unsalted butter, melted and cooled

1 teaspoon pure vanilla extract

½ cup sour cream

⅔ cup unsweetened cocoa powder

2¼ cups all-purpose flour

1½ teaspoons baking soda

1½ teaspoons baking powder

1 teaspoon kosher salt

2 cups packed grated fresh pears, from about 3 medium pears

4 ounces semisweet chocolate, melted and cooled

Glaze

1 cup confectioners' sugar

2 tablespoons smooth pear sauce or applesauce

2 tablespoons whole milk

1 teaspoon pure vanilla extract

Kosher salt

Ground cinnamon

1. MAKE THE CAKE: Preheat the oven to 325°F with a rack in the center position. Grease a sheet pan with nonstick spray.

2. In a large bowl, vigorously whisk together the eggs, brown sugar, and granulated sugar until pale and foamy, about 1 minute. Whisk in the oil, melted butter, vanilla, and sour cream until smooth. Sift in the cocoa powder, flour, baking soda, baking powder, and salt and mix with a wooden spoon or rubber spatula until the batter just comes together. Fold in the grated pears and melted chocolate until well combined.

3. Pour the batter into the prepared pan and spread it evenly to the corners with a large offset spatula. Bake for 15 to 20 minutes, until the cake is springy and a tester inserted into the center comes out clean. Allow the cake to cool completely in the pan, about 25 minutes.

4. MEANWHILE, MAKE THE GLAZE: In a medium bowl, whisk together the confectioners' sugar, pear sauce, milk, vanilla, and a pinch each of salt and cinnamon until smooth and pourable.

5. Spread the glaze thinly over the cooled cake and let it set for about 10 minutes before slicing and serving. The cake will keep, tightly covered, at room temperature for up to 3 days.

Triple Citrus Poke Cake

SERVES 24

Ever made a poke cake before? They became popular in the 1970s, and were often made with a box of Jell-O—my version is a bit more updated and homemade. It's pretty much what it sounds like. Yes, you will be deliberately poking holes into your freshly baked cake, but only so you can then fill those holes with a sweet, citrusy glaze that helps bring beautiful moisture and vibrant, craveable flavor to the finished cake. Lemons, oranges, and limes flavor this bright beauty— it's a great pick-me-up both in the heat of summer and on chilly winter days.

Nonstick cooking spray

3⅓ cups all-purpose flour

1¼ teaspoons baking powder

1 teaspoon baking soda

1¼ teaspoons kosher salt

2½ cups granulated sugar

Zest of 1 lemon

Zest of 1 orange

1¼ cups (2½ sticks) unsalted butter, at room temperature

1⅔ cups whole milk

¼ cup fresh lemon juice

¼ cup fresh orange juice

5 large eggs

Zest of 2 limes

½ cup fresh lime juice

2 cups plus 2 tablespoons confectioners' sugar

2 cups heavy cream

1. Preheat the oven to 350°F with a rack in the center position. Grease a sheet pan with nonstick spray.

2. In a medium bowl, whisk together the flour, baking powder, baking soda, and salt.

3. In the bowl of a stand mixer fitted with the paddle attachment or in a large bowl with a handheld mixer, beat the granulated sugar with both zests until fragrant, 3 to 5 minutes. Add the butter and beat until light and fluffy, about 5 minutes.

4. In a large, spouted measuring cup, stir together the milk, lemon juice, and orange juice. Set aside to curdle for 5 minutes.

5. Add the eggs to the sugar mixture one at a time, mixing well on medium speed and scraping down the sides of the bowl after each addition. Add about half the flour mixture and mix on low speed to incorporate. Add the milk–citrus juice mixture and mix until almost fully incorporated, then add the remaining flour mixture and mix just until the batter comes together.

6. Pour the batter into the prepared pan and spread it evenly to the corners. Bake for 25 to 30 minutes, until the cake starts to pull away from the sides of the pan and a tester inserted into the center comes out clean. Transfer the pan to a wire rack, then use a skewer or toothpick to poke small holes all over, about ½ inch apart.

7. In a large, spouted measuring cup, whisk together the lime zest, lime juice, and 2 cups of the confectioners' sugar. Carefully pour the glaze evenly over the still-warm cake, letting it drip down into the holes. Allow the cake to cool fully in the pan, about 25 minutes.

8. Just before serving, in the bowl of a stand mixer fitted with the whisk attachment or in a large bowl with a handheld mixer, whip together the cream and remaining 2 tablespoons confectioners' sugar on medium speed until it holds medium-firm peaks, about 3 minutes. Either slather the whipped cream over the cake like frosting, or slice the cake and serve each piece with a healthy dollop of whipped cream on top. Without the cream, the cake will keep, tightly covered, in the refrigerator for 4 to 5 days; with the cream on top, it will keep for just a day or two.

German's Chocolate Crater Cake

SERVES 24

This is my riff on an earthquake cake—typically boxed cake mix baked with dollops of sweet cream cheese batter until a gooey, craggy, crater-y dessert emerges from the oven. A marriage of sheet cake, cheesecake, and molten lava cake, my version is gussied up with coconut and pecans, and begs to be scooped from the pan warm and topped with a cool spoonful of vanilla ice cream and a drizzle of homemade or store-bought caramel sauce to complete that German's chocolate flavor trifecta. If you'd like to play around with flavors, you can omit the coconut and/or swap the pecans for another type of nut—almonds or peanuts would be divine.

Cake

Nonstick cooking spray

2 cups unsweetened coconut flakes, toasted (see headnote, page 33), plus more for topping

1 cup roughly chopped pecans, plus more for topping

1¾ cups all-purpose flour

2 cups granulated sugar

¾ cup unsweetened cocoa powder

1 tablespoon instant espresso powder (optional)

2 teaspoons baking soda

1 teaspoon baking powder

1 teaspoon kosher salt

1 cup buttermilk

½ cup vegetable oil

4 large eggs

2 teaspoons pure vanilla extract

1 cup boiling water

Topping

1 (8-ounce) package cream cheese, at room temperature

½ cup (1 stick) unsalted butter, melted

3 cups confectioners' sugar

1 teaspoon pure vanilla extract

Kosher salt

Vanilla ice cream, for serving (optional)

Caramel sauce, store-bought or homemade (see page 100), for serving (optional)

1. MAKE THE CAKE: Preheat the oven to 350°F with a rack in the center position. Grease a sheet pan with nonstick spray.

2. Scatter the coconut flakes and chopped pecans evenly over the bottom of the prepared pan.

3. In a large bowl, sift together the flour, granulated sugar, cocoa powder, espresso powder, if using, baking soda, baking powder, and salt.

4. In a medium bowl, whisk together the buttermilk, oil, eggs, and vanilla until smooth.

5. Add the wet ingredients to the dry and whisk gently until a smooth batter comes together. Stir in the boiling water until smooth.

6. Pour the cake batter evenly onto the prepared pan.

7. MAKE THE TOPPING: In the bowl of a stand mixer fitted with the paddle attachment or in a large bowl using a handheld mixer, beat together the cream cheese, butter, confectioners' sugar, vanilla, and a pinch of salt until smooth.

8. Dollop and drizzle the cream cheese mixture over the batter, letting it pool and sink in places. Top with extra coconut and pecans. Bake for 20 to 25 minutes, until the chocolate part of the cake is puffed and dry (a tester inserted into the center will not come out clean). Let the cake cool in the pan for about 10 minutes.

9. Scoop out portions of cake and serve warm, topped with scoops of ice cream and a drizzle of caramel sauce. The cake will keep, tightly covered, in the refrigerator for up to 4 days. Warm slices in the microwave for 15 to 20 seconds before serving.

Neapolitan Cake

SERVES 24

Like the marble cake on page 30, here's another "one batter, several flavors" situation, this time with the classic Neapolitan ice cream combination of chocolate, vanilla, and strawberry. We'll use freeze-dried strawberries, crushed into a fine powder, for that punch of pink, and you can either make a block-striped tricolor cake (to match that beloved box of ice cream) or marble all the flavors together—that way, you get bites of each flavor in each slice of cake. The frosting mirrors the cake in both whimsical flavor and simple technique, so swoop it on generously and revel in the bliss of having it all—all three flavors and no threat of melting, I mean.

Cake

Nonstick baking spray

1 cup (2 sticks) unsalted butter, at room temperature

1¾ cups granulated sugar

5 large eggs

3 cups all-purpose flour

2½ teaspoons baking powder

½ teaspoon kosher salt

1¼ cups whole milk

¼ cup vegetable oil

1 tablespoon pure vanilla extract

¼ cup unsweetened cocoa powder

1 (1.2-ounce) package dried strawberries, finely crushed into a powder (about 6 tablespoons)

Frosting

1 (8-ounce) package cream cheese, at room temperature

½ cup (1 stick) unsalted butter, at room temperature

3 cups confectioners' sugar

1 tablespoon pure vanilla extract

1 tablespoon unsweetened cocoa powder

1. MAKE THE CAKE: Preheat the oven to 350°F with a rack in the center position. Grease a sheet pan with nonstick spray.

2. In the bowl of a stand mixer fitted with the paddle attachment or in a large bowl with a handheld mixer, beat together the butter and granulated sugar on medium-high speed until fluffy and combined, about 3 minutes. Add the eggs one at a time, beating until smooth and scraping down the sides of the bowl after each addition.

3. In a medium bowl, whisk together the flour, baking powder, and salt.

4. In a large, spouted measuring cup, mix together the milk, oil, and vanilla.

5. With the mixer running on low speed, alternate adding the dry ingredients and the wet ingredients to the egg mixture, beginning and ending with the dry ingredients and scraping down the sides of the bowl as needed, until a smooth batter comes together.

6. Divide the batter evenly among three separate bowls (you can leave one-third in the mixing bowl—this is the vanilla batter). Sift the cocoa powder into one of the bowls and gently fold until well combined—this is the chocolate batter. Gently fold 4½ tablespoons of the freeze-dried strawberry powder into the remaining bowl— this is the strawberry batter.

7. For a block-striped cake, spread each flavor separately over a third of the prepared pan with a small offset spatula to achieve three thick, distinct stripes. For a marbled look, scoop the batter from each bowl in random blobs over the pan, covering it to the

recipe continues

corners, then spread and swirl a knife or small offset spatula through the batter several times to push it to the edges of the pan and achieve a marble pattern. Bake for 20 to 25 minutes, until the cake starts to pull away from the sides of the pan and a tester inserted into the center comes out clean. Allow the cake to cool completely in the pan, about 25 minutes.

8. MEANWHILE, MAKE THE FROSTING: In the bowl of a stand mixer fitted with the paddle attachment or in a large bowl using a handheld mixer, beat together the cream cheese and butter on medium-high speed until smooth and fluffy, about 5 minutes. Add the confectioners' sugar and vanilla and beat on low speed to incorporate. Increase the mixer speed to high and beat the frosting until smooth and bright white in color, about 5 minutes.

9. Divide the frosting evenly among three separate bowls (you can leave one-third of it in the mixing bowl—this is the vanilla frosting). Whisk the cocoa powder into another bowl—this is the chocolate frosting. Stir the remaining 1½ tablespoons strawberry powder into the remaining bowl—this is the strawberry frosting.

10. For a striped look, spread each frosting flavor thickly over its corresponding cake flavor. For a marbled look, dollop each flavor of frosting randomly over the cooled cake, covering it to the corners, then swoop a toothpick or skewer throughout the frosting for a swirled, marbled effect.

11. Slice into pieces and serve. The cake will keep, tightly covered, in the refrigerator for up to 4 days.

Giant Flag Cake

SERVES 24

Every year on July Fourth, my sister Emily decorates a giant vanilla cake to look like the American flag—colorful and festive, it's always a big hit and feeds everyone at the BBQ. Emily usually uses Ina Garten's recipe; while I think we can all agree that Ina is the queen and her taste impeccable, I wanted a one-bowl flag cake that could be made with just a whisk, plus a lightened-up frosting to pair perfectly with the decorative red and blue berries on top. Here's my version.

Cake

Nonstick cooking spray

6 large eggs, at room temperature

2½ cups granulated sugar

½ cup (1 stick) unsalted butter, melted and cooled

1 cup canola oil

2 cups buttermilk

1 tablespoon pure vanilla extract

¼ teaspoon pure almond extract

4 cups all-purpose flour

1 tablespoon baking powder

1 teaspoon baking soda

1 teaspoon kosher salt

Frosting and Decorating

2 cups heavy cream, cold

1 cup plain full-fat Greek yogurt

½ cup confectioners' sugar

Zest of 1 lemon

1 tablespoon pure vanilla extract

1 pint fresh blueberries

1 pint fresh strawberries, hulled and sliced ¼ inch thick

1 pint fresh raspberries

1. MAKE THE CAKE: Preheat the oven to 350°F with a rack in the center position. Grease a sheet pan with nonstick spray.

2. In a large bowl, vigorously whisk together the eggs and granulated sugar for 1 minute, until well combined and very frothy. Whisk in the melted butter, oil, buttermilk, vanilla, and almond extract until smooth.

3. Add the flour, baking powder, baking soda, and salt. Gently fold with the whisk until the batter is smooth and streak-free.

4. Pour the batter into the prepared pan and spread it evenly to the corners with a large offset spatula. Bake for 18 to 20 minutes, until the cake is golden and pulls away from the sides of the pan and a tester inserted into the center comes out clean. Run a paring knife around the edges of the cake to loosen and then allow the cake to cool completely in the pan, about 25 minutes.

5. MEANWHILE, MAKE THE FROSTING: In the bowl of a stand mixer fitted with the whisk attachment or in a large bowl with a handheld mixer, whip together the cream, yogurt, and sugar until medium-stiff peaks form, about 3 minutes. Add the lemon zest and vanilla and whisk until stiff peaks form, about 2 minutes more.

6. Spread the frosting in a thick, even layer over the cake. Use a toothpick or small offset spatula to faintly outline the shape of the American flag in the frosting to guide you as you decorate. Arrange the blueberries in the upper left corner as the "stars," and make red stripes by arranging double rows of raspberries and/or overlapping strawberry slices over the rest of the cake.

7. Chill the cake in the refrigerator, uncovered, until ready to serve. The cake will keep, tightly covered, in the refrigerator for up to 3 days.

photograph follows

Nana's Christmas Gingerbread

SERVES 24

I met Ben's Nana Peggy in the last year of her life, when she was ninety-two years old. A true Southern lady and generous in every way, Nana's recipes weren't complete without sticks (plural) of butter, shortening, and cream. She made a habit of tall and creamy pies, fried chicken, cheese biscuits, lush layer cakes, and cornbread. Her recipe journals are rich and full of whimsy—reading them now helps fill in the gaps for me, a friend who came late into her life. This gingerbread recipe is one of several of Nana's that I make every year. It's sweet and spicy and utterly lovely, its texture akin to the fluffiest, springiest layer cake. I love that this gingerbread is heavy enough with spice to evoke the season, yet light enough in texture to follow a rich holiday meal. It needs nothing more than a generous dusting of confectioners' sugar on top before serving, but in the spirit of Peggy (more is more), feel free to dollop it with some lightly sweetened whipped cream or even a scoop of ice cream, if you like.

Nonstick baking spray

2⅔ cups all-purpose flour

2 tablespoons ground cinnamon

2 tablespoons ground ginger

1½ teaspoons ground allspice

¾ teaspoon ground nutmeg

¾ teaspoon kosher salt

4 large eggs

1⅓ cups granulated sugar

1⅓ cups unsulfured molasses

1⅓ cups canola oil

2 teaspoons baking soda, dissolved in 3 tablespoons hot water

1 cup boiling water

Confectioners' sugar

Vanilla ice cream, for serving (optional)

1. Preheat the oven to 325°F with a rack in the center position. Grease a sheet pan with nonstick spray.

2. In a medium bowl, whisk together the flour, cinnamon, ginger, allspice, nutmeg, and salt.

3. In a large bowl, whisk together the eggs and granulated sugar until smooth. Whisk in the molasses to combine, then slowly add the oil, whisking continuously to incorporate. Whisk in the dissolved baking soda.

4. Add the dry ingredients to the wet ingredients and whisk well to combine. Pour in the boiling water and beat lightly and quickly until incorporated (the batter will be very wet—that's okay!).

5. Pour the batter into the prepared pan and spread it evenly to the corners with a large offset spatula. Bake for about 28 minutes, until the cake starts to pull away from the sides of the pan and a tester inserted into the center comes out clean. Allow the cake to cool completely in the pan, about 25 minutes.

6. Before serving, dust with confectioners' sugar and slice into pieces. The cake will keep, tightly covered, in the refrigerator for up to a week.

Double Chocolate Sheet Cake

SERVES 24

This ultimate chocolate cake is for all of my fellow chocolate super-fans out there. A combination of buttermilk, oil, and hot coffee give this cake a perfectly dense yet springy texture with rich chocolate flavor throughout. Whipped ganache is the literal frosting on top of this simple bit of chocolate perfection. If it were socially acceptable, I'd eat the entire pan by myself, Bruce Bogtrotter–style. Alas, my youngest son tells me that "sharing is caring," so here we are.

Cake

- Nonstick cooking spray
- 1¾ cups all-purpose flour
- 2 cups sugar
- ¾ cup unsweetened cocoa powder
- 2 teaspoons baking soda
- 1 teaspoon baking powder
- 1 teaspoon kosher salt
- 1 cup buttermilk
- ½ cup vegetable oil
- 4 large eggs
- 2 teaspoons pure vanilla extract
- 1 cup hot brewed coffee

Frosting

- 1 cup heavy cream
- 10 ounces bittersweet chocolate chips

1. MAKE THE CAKE: Preheat the oven to 350°F with a rack in the center position. Grease a sheet pan with nonstick spray.

2. In a large bowl, sift together the flour, sugar, cocoa powder, baking soda, baking powder, and salt.

3. In a medium bowl, whisk together the buttermilk, oil, eggs, and vanilla until smooth.

4. Add the wet ingredients to the dry ingredients and whisk gently until a smooth batter comes together. Gently stir in the hot coffee until smooth.

5. Pour the batter into the prepared pan and spread it evenly to the corners with a large offset spatula. Bake for 12 to 15 minutes, until the cake starts to pull away from the sides of the pan and a tester inserted into the center comes out just clean. Allow the cake to cool completely in the pan, about 20 minutes.

6. MEANWHILE, MAKE THE FROSTING: Warm the cream in a small saucepan over medium heat (or in 20-second increments in the microwave) until just starting to steam. Place the chocolate chips in a large bowl. Pour the hot cream over the chocolate chips and let the mixture sit, undisturbed, for 3 minutes to melt, then whisk until glossy and smooth. Let the ganache cool at room temperature until thick but still soft, about 15 minutes. Whip with a handheld mixer on medium-high speed until light and fluffy, about 5 minutes.

7. Spread the whipped ganache over the cooled cake in swoops and swirls. Slice and serve. The cake will keep, tightly covered, in the refrigerator for up to a week.

Pumpkin Cake

with Brown Butter Frosting

SERVES 24

If the very first fallen leaves of autumn bring out your desire to bake everything *pumpkin*, you're definitely not alone. This warmly spiced pumpkin cake screams fall, so pull out those cable-knit sweaters, tall boots, and spiced lattes! Pumpkin patch photo shoot! ALL THE BUFFALO PLAID! Truth be told, this cake is just as amazing in the winter or spring. The creamy, nutty brown butter frosting really takes this cake from ordinary to extraordinary. I adapted the recipe from one by Adrianna Adarme at A Cozy Kitchen, and if you haven't checked out her work yet, you're in for a treat.

Cake

Nonstick cooking spray

4 large eggs

1 cup packed brown sugar

1 cup granulated sugar

2 cups canned pure pumpkin puree

1 cup vegetable oil

1 teaspoon kosher salt

2 teaspoons ground cinnamon

1 teaspoon ground ginger

½ teaspoon ground allspice

½ teaspoon ground nutmeg

3 cups all-purpose flour

2 teaspoons baking powder

1 teaspoon baking soda

Frosting

1½ cups (3 sticks) unsalted butter, at room temperature

4 cups confectioners' sugar

1 teaspoon pure vanilla extract

Kosher salt

2 tablespoons whole milk or heavy cream

1. MAKE THE CAKE: Preheat the oven to 325°F with a rack in the center position. Grease a sheet pan with nonstick spray.

2. In a large bowl, vigorously whisk together the eggs, brown sugar, and granulated sugar until light and frothy, about 1 minute. Whisk in the pumpkin puree, oil, salt, cinnamon, ginger, allspice, nutmeg, flour, baking powder, and baking soda until a smooth, streak-free batter comes together.

3. Pour the batter into the prepared pan and spread it evenly to the corners with a large offset spatula. Bake for about 30 minutes, until the cake is springy and a tester inserted in the center comes out clean. Allow the cake to cool completely in the pan, about 25 minutes.

4. MAKE THE FROSTING: Melt 1 cup (2 sticks) of the butter in a medium saucepan over medium heat. Cook about 5 minutes, stirring often, until the butter turns a toasted, amber color (it will bubble and spit; when it quiets down, check for browning). Pour the brown butter into a small, freezer-safe bowl, making sure to scrape the pan for all those delicious browned bits, then chill the butter in the freezer for about 20 minutes, until it has cooled and firmed up a bit.

5. In the bowl of a stand mixer fitted with the paddle attachment or in a large bowl with a handheld mixer, cream the brown butter, remaining ½ cup (1 stick) butter, the confectioners' sugar, and vanilla on medium-high speed until smooth, 3 to 5 minutes. Add a pinch of salt and the milk and beat until the frosting has lightened in color and is quite fluffy, 2 to 3 minutes.

6. Spread the frosting over the cooled cake, then cut into pieces and serve. The cake will keep, tightly covered, in the refrigerator for up to 4 days.

Cannoli Icebox Cake

SERVES 24

Growing up in Philadelphia, there was no shortage of good Italian-American bakeries to choose from, and plenty of cannoli to go around. My memories of childhood bakery trips involve lots of cannoli shell towers piled high, waiting for their fresh cream fillings. This fuss-free no-bake cake comes together in a flash and serves fresh cannoli vibes without your having to fry up shells and stuff them to order. The cake layers are made with sweet ricotta and graham crackers, and the crackers soften to a cakelike consistency after a few hours (or a night) in the refrigerator. Mini chocolate chips and orange zest round out that cannoli flavor, though if you wanted to add some chopped pistachios and/or candied orange peel to the mix, I'm sure that would be delicious. If you don't have room in the fridge for a regular sheet pan, this recipe can easily be halved to fit on a quarter sheet.

16 ounces whole-milk ricotta

2 cups heavy cream, cold

½ cup confectioners' sugar

½ teaspoon ground cinnamon

2 teaspoons pure vanilla extract

Zest of 1 orange

½ cup mini chocolate chips, plus more for topping

36 whole graham crackers (from 4 sleeves)

1. In the bowl of a stand mixer fitted with the whisk attachment or in a large bowl with a handheld mixer, whip together the ricotta, cream, confectioners' sugar, cinnamon, vanilla, and orange zest on medium-high speed until stiff peaks form, 3 to 5 minutes.

2. Spread a very thin layer of the cream mixture over the bottom of a sheet pan with a large offset spatula (this will help the first layer of graham crackers stick). Arrange a single layer of graham crackers over the cream, breaking up the crackers to fill any holes and reach all the way to the corners.

3. Fold the chocolate chips into the remaining cream mixture in the bowl with a rubber spatula, then spread a thick layer of cream on top of the graham crackers. Top with another layer of graham crackers, then the remaining cream. Finish with more chocolate chips and any extra graham crackers, crushed up into small pieces.

4. Cover the pan with plastic wrap and let it rest in the refrigerator for at least 2 hours, or up to overnight—the graham crackers will soften in the cream and get "cakey."

5. Slice or scoop the cake into large pieces and serve. It will keep, tightly covered, in the refrigerator for up to 2 days.

How Do I: **Switch Up the Flavors in This Cake?**

Love an icebox cake but not feeling the cannoli vibes? That's okay! It's easy to switch up the flavor profile of this simple cake. For a Black Forest icebox cake, use chocolate graham crackers or wafer cookies, skip the cinnamon and orange zest, and fold a half cup of cherry preserves and some chopped, dried cherries into the cream mixture. For a banana cream cake, use Nilla wafer cookies alongside the graham crackers, omit the orange zest and chocolate chips, and add thin slices of fresh banana on top of the cookie layer. For a simple snickerdoodle icebox cake, use cinnamon grahams, swap 2 tablespoons of the confectioners' sugar for brown sugar, and skip the orange zest and chocolate chips—decorate the top of the cake with a healthy dose of cinnamon sugar instead.

Layered & Rolled Cakes

A Little Bit Fancy

One of the wonderful things about baking cake on a sheet pan is the opportunity to quickly and easily make beautiful layered or rolled cakes. So yes, now we're getting a liiiiittle bit fancy, but I promise there's nothing too difficult or intimidating about stacking cake layers or even coaxing a spongy sheet cake into an elegant little roll.

I know, I know, you're thinking: *Rolled* cakes? Like roulades? Swiss rolls? Who am I, Paul Hollywood? Albert freaking Einstein? And the answer is yes! Roll up your cakes! Do it while they're still warm, when they're nice and flexible. With just a little confectioners' sugar and a clean dish towel, in this chapter I'll show you how. Just you wait—in no time flat, you'll be serving up a Strawberry & Cream Roll (page 64), a Sticky Toffee Date Roll (page 61), or a Chocolate Hazelnut Bûche de Noël (page 58), and you'll have Mr. Hollywood on speed dial.

Cutting cake layers from a sheet cake is a no-brainer, and I can't believe it took me upward of thirty-five long years to figure it out. All we do is cut circles or rectangles from our giant sheet cake, then simply frost, stack, and decorate them as we like! We just need one pan, instead of two, three, or even four different pans! The cake cools so quickly! And we can even use the leftover cake scraps to adorn our towering layers with piles of sweet crumbs or bouncy cake cubes. So whether you're craving something classic, like Sunny Sprinkle Layer Cake (page 87) or Red Velvet Cake with White Chocolate Frosting (page 89), or are looking for something more off the beaten path, like Maple Butternut Cake (page 69), I've got you covered, and this is going to be fun.

Chocolate Hazelnut Bûche de Noël

SERVES 8 TO 10

Who doesn't love a good bûche? These log-shaped Christmas cakes are popular the world over, and there are so many different ways to flavor and decorate them. I'm partial to the bewitching combination of chocolate and hazelnut, so you'll find some hazelnut flour in the cake batter and a good bit of chocolate hazelnut spread in the smooth, creamy filling. As for decorating, I like to keep it fairly simple and forgo the traditional meringue mushrooms (the holidays are busy enough, amirite?) for a cocoa-dusted display of the gorgeous sponge swirl "bump" on the log, and a scattering of whole hazelnuts for extra woodsy vibes.

Note: If you can't find hazelnut flour (sometimes called hazelnut meal) at the store, you can make your own by blitzing whole hazelnuts in a high-speed blender or food processor just until soft and finely ground. (Be careful of overprocessing; if you blitz for too long, you'll end up with hazelnut butter!)

Cake

Nonstick cooking spray
¾ cup hazelnut flour
¼ cup all-purpose flour
¼ teaspoon kosher salt
1 teaspoon baking powder
5 large eggs
¾ cup granulated sugar
1 teaspoon pure vanilla extract
Confectioners' sugar

Filling

1 cup chocolate hazelnut spread, such as Nutella
8 ounces mascarpone cheese

Decorating

Handful of whole hazelnuts
Cocoa powder

1. MAKE THE CAKE: Preheat the oven to 400°F with a rack in the center position. Grease a sheet pan with nonstick spray, line it with parchment paper, and grease the parchment, too.

2. In a medium bowl, whisk together the hazelnut flour, all-purpose flour, salt, and baking powder.

3. In the bowl of a stand mixer fitted with the whisk attachment or in a large bowl with a handheld mixer, whip the eggs and granulated sugar together on high speed until pale yellow and thick, about 5 minutes. Mix in the vanilla, then add the flour mixture and mix on low speed until combined.

4. Pour the batter into the prepared pan and spread it evenly to the corners with a large offset spatula. Bake until the cake springs back when lightly poked, 6 to 8 minutes.

5. While the cake bakes, lay a clean dish towel on a work surface and fill a fine-mesh sieve with about ½ cup confectioners' sugar.

6. Remove the cake from the oven and immediately run a paring knife around the edges of the pan to loosen the cake. Working quickly, while the cake is still hot, sift a thick layer of confectioners' sugar over the top, then turn the cake out of the pan onto the dish towel, sugared side down. Carefully remove the baked-on parchment from the cake, then sprinkle a layer of confectioners' sugar where the parchment used to be. Gently roll up the cake and the towel, starting from a short side and rolling away from yourself. Let the cake cool completely in the towel, about 30 minutes.

7. MEANWHILE, MAKE THE FILLING: In the bowl of a stand mixer fitted with the whisk attachment or in a large bowl with a handheld mixer, whip together the chocolate hazelnut spread and mascarpone on high speed until fluffy and well combined, 3 to 5 minutes.

recipe continues

8. When the cake is cool, unroll it onto a work surface. Keeping a few tablespoons aside for decorating, spread the chocolate hazelnut filling thickly over the cake, leaving a ½-inch border. Tightly but gently roll up the cake with the filling inside (this time leave the towel behind). Use a serrated knife to trim the ends of the roll to make neat edges. Carefully slice a 2-inch section from one end of the cake, angling the knife about 45 degrees (this piece of cake will become the little bump on the yule log). Transfer the large "log" to a serving platter, seam side down, then use the leftover chocolate hazelnut filling to adhere the bump, angled side up, to the top of the log.

9. DECORATE THE CAKE: Arrange the hazelnuts on and around the log, then sprinkle the top of the cake lightly with cocoa powder. Cut the cake into thick slices to serve. The cake will keep, loosely covered, in the refrigerator for 2 to 3 days.

How Do I: **Substitute for Mascarpone Cheese?**

Mascarpone cheese is a fresh, spreadable, Italian double cream cheese, and its thick, creamy richness brings both wonderful flavor and texture to many recipes in this book—I particularly love it for punching up and stabilizing a cream filling. If you can't find mascarpone at your local market, though, you could happily use regular cream cheese instead. Better yet, mix a spoonful of sour cream or plain Greek yogurt into your cream cheese, and you'll better replicate the soft, creamy texture and slight tang of true mascarpone.

Sticky Toffee Date Roll

SERVES 8 TO 10

There are three essential parts to this sweet and sophisticated roll: A close-textured date sponge, a thick vanilla cream, and a sticky, salted toffee sauce. Each element is special on its own, but combined? Divine. Though I admit this cake involves a bit more work than some of the others (we make our own date puree, mix up the sponge, whip up the cream, and then simmer the toffee sauce until perfectly thick and smooth), none of the steps are difficult, and the final product—a towering roll of sweet, salty, creamy magnificence—is worth the fuss.

Cake

Nonstick cooking spray

1½ cups pitted dates, preferably Medjool

Boiling water

1 cup all-purpose flour

1 teaspoon ground cinnamon

½ teaspoon baking soda

½ teaspoon kosher salt

5 large eggs

½ cup granulated sugar

½ cup packed brown sugar

Confectioners' sugar

Filling

1 cup heavy cream, cold

8 ounces mascarpone cheese

½ cup granulated sugar

1 teaspoon pure vanilla extract

Kosher salt

Toffee Sauce

½ cup (1 stick) unsalted butter

6 tablespoons heavy cream

½ cup packed brown sugar

1 teaspoon kosher salt

1. MAKE THE CAKE: Preheat the oven to 350°F with a rack in the center position. Grease a sheet pan with nonstick spray, line it with parchment, and grease the parchment, too.

2. Place the dates in a medium heatproof bowl and pour boiling water over to cover. Let the dates soak and absorb the water for 10 minutes, then use an immersion blender (or transfer to a standing blender) to puree until smooth.

3. In a medium bowl, whisk together the flour, cinnamon, baking soda, and salt.

4. In the bowl of a stand mixer fitted with the whisk attachment or in a large bowl with a handheld mixer, whip the eggs, granulated sugar, and brown sugar together on high speed until light yellow and doubled in volume, about 5 minutes. Mix in the date puree until smooth, then fold in the dry ingredients with a rubber spatula until the batter comes together without any streaks.

5. Pour the batter into the prepared pan and spread it evenly to the corners with a large offset spatula. Bake for about 15 minutes, until the cake is well browned and springs back when gently poked in the center.

6. While the cake bakes, lay a clean dish towel on a work surface and fill a fine-mesh sieve with about ½ cup confectioners' sugar.

7. Remove the cake from the oven and immediately run a paring knife around the edges of the pan to loosen the cake. Working quickly while the cake is still hot, sift a thin layer of confectioners' sugar over the cake, then turn the cake out of the pan onto the dish towel, sugared side down. Carefully remove the baked-on parchment from the cake, then sprinkle a layer of confectioners' sugar where the parchment used to be. Gently roll up the cake and the towel, starting from a short side and rolling away from yourself. Let the cake cool completely in the towel, about 35 minutes.

recipe continues

8. MEANWHILE, MAKE THE FILLING: In a large bowl, whisk together the cream, mascarpone, granulated sugar, vanilla, and a pinch of salt until thick, smooth, and spreadable.

9. MAKE THE TOFFEE SAUCE: In a small saucepan, warm the butter, cream, brown sugar, and salt over medium heat until melted and smooth, about 5 minutes. Bring to a simmer and cook for 3 to 5 minutes, stirring gently, until the sauce coats the back of a spoon. Remove from the heat and allow to cool.

10. Once the cake is cool, unroll it onto a work surface. Spread the cream filling over the cake, leaving a ½-inch border. Tightly but gently roll up the cake with the filling inside (this time leave the towel behind). If you'd like, use a serrated knife to trim the ends of the roll to make neat edges. Carefully transfer the cake to a serving platter, seam side down.

11. Pour the toffee sauce over the cake. Immediately cut the cake into thick slices to serve. The cake will keep, tightly covered, in the refrigerator for up to 3 days.

Strawberry & Cream Roll

SERVES 8 TO 10

This cake gets its bright yet delicate strawberry flavor from both freeze-dried strawberries and strawberry jam. Paired with a smooth mascarpone cream, this gorgeous cake is ready for anything from your next pink princess-themed birthday party to breakfast at Wimbledon.

1 (1.2-ounce) package dried strawberries, finely crushed into a powder (about 6 tablespoons)

Cake

Nonstick cooking spray

¾ cup cake flour

¼ teaspoon kosher salt

1 teaspoon baking powder

5 large eggs

¾ cup granulated sugar

1 teaspoon pure vanilla extract

Red or pink food coloring (optional)

Confectioners' sugar

Filling

8 ounces mascarpone cheese

1 cup heavy cream, cold

¾ cup confectioners' sugar

1 teaspoon pure vanilla extract

Red or pink food coloring (optional)

Scant ½ cup strawberry jam

1. MAKE THE CAKE: Preheat the oven to 400°F with a rack in the center position. Grease a sheet pan with nonstick spray, line it with parchment paper, and grease the parchment, too.

2. In a medium bowl, whisk together 4 tablespoons of the strawberry powder, the cake flour, salt, and baking powder.

3. In the bowl of a stand mixer fitted with the whisk attachment or in a large bowl with a handheld mixer, whip the eggs and granulated sugar together on high speed until light yellow and doubled in volume, about 5 minutes. Whip in the vanilla and 1 or 2 drops of red food coloring, if using. Add the flour mixture in two additions, whipping on low speed just to combine and scraping down the sides of the bowl with a rubber spatula after each addition.

4. Pour the batter into the prepared pan and spread it evenly to the corners with a large offset spatula. Bake for 5 to 7 minutes, until the cake is just golden and springs back when lightly poked.

5. While the cake bakes, lay a clean dish towel on a work surface and fill a fine-mesh sieve with about ½ cup confectioners' sugar.

6. Remove the cake from the oven and immediately run a paring knife around the edges of the pan to loosen the cake. Working quickly while the cake is still hot, sift a thin layer of confectioners' sugar over the cake, then turn the cake out of the pan onto the dish towel, sugared side down. Carefully remove the baked-on parchment from the cake, then sprinkle a layer of confectioners' sugar where the parchment used to be. Gently roll up the cake and the towel, starting from a short side and rolling away from yourself. Let the cake cool completely in the towel, about 35 minutes.

7. MEANWHILE, MAKE THE FILLING: In the bowl of a stand mixer fitted with the whisk attachment or in a large bowl with a handheld mixer, whip together the mascarpone, cream, and confectioners' sugar on medium-high speed until beginning to thicken, about 3 minutes. Add the remaining 2 tablespoons strawberry powder, the vanilla, and a drop of red food coloring, if using, and whip until thick and smooth, about 2 minutes more.

8. When the cake is cool, unroll it onto a work surface. Spread the strawberry jam thinly over the cake, leaving a ½-inch border, then spread the mascarpone cream evenly over the jam. Tightly but gently roll up the cake with the filling inside (this time leave the towel behind). If you'd like, use a serrated knife to trim the ends of the roulade to make neat edges. Carefully transfer the cake to a serving platter, seam side down.

9. Sprinkle the roulade with a bit of confectioners' sugar, then cut the cake into thick slices to serve. The cake will keep, loosely covered, in the refrigerator for 2 to 3 days.

Tell Me: **What Exactly Is Freeze-Dried Fruit?**

Freeze-dried fruit is just fruit that has undergone a complicated process to remove its moisture, rendering it crispy, dry, and shelf-stable—and particularly useful in baking. Using freeze-dried fruit allows us to achieve concentrated, fresh fruit flavor, without introducing extra moisture to our cake batters, fillings, or buttercreams (extra moisture that might cause these things to weep or refuse to rise properly). Unopened bags of freeze-dried fruit last for many months in the pantry, and they're highly swappable, flavor-wise. If you don't have freeze-dried strawberries for this Strawberry & Cream Roll, for example, you could easily use freeze-dried raspberries, blueberries, or even mangoes instead.

photograph follows

Victoria's Really Quite Large Sponge

SERVES 20

Like everyone else with a television, I became enamored with The Great British Baking Show *(or* The Great British Bake Off, *depending on where you live) when it first hit the airwaves on this side of the pond. The accents! The baked goods! The gentle and genuine camaraderie! The ever-present jokes about soggy bottoms! Sigh. Watching an episode was like a balm for the soul, especially during the most stressful days of 2020's lockdown. Watching GBBO is where I first learned about the Victoria sponge, a simple English sandwich cake held together with jam and cream. Apparently a favorite of Queen Victoria, for whom the cake was named, the "Vicky sponge" is a British teatime favorite, though this American is chuffed by a slice at any hour. This extra-large sheet pan version is a lovely treat for a baby shower, bridal brunch, or book club gathering.*

Nonstick cooking spray

1⅔ cups cake flour

1 tablespoon baking powder

1 teaspoon kosher salt

1¼ cups (2½ sticks) unsalted butter, at room temperature

1 cup granulated sugar

1 teaspoon pure vanilla extract

5 large eggs

1½ cups heavy cream, cold

2 tablespoons confectioners' sugar, plus more for dusting

2 tablespoons crème fraîche or plain yogurt

¾ cup raspberry jam

1. MAKE THE CAKE: Preheat the oven to 350°F with a rack in the center position. Grease a sheet pan with nonstick spray, line it with parchment paper, and grease the parchment, too.

2. In a medium bowl, whisk the flour, baking powder, and salt.

3. In the bowl of a stand mixer fitted with the paddle attachment or in a large bowl with a handheld mixer, cream together the butter and granulated sugar on medium-high speed until fluffy and light, 3 to 5 minutes. Beat in the vanilla, then add the eggs one at a time, beating well and adding a small spoonful of the flour mixture after each addition. Once the eggs are incorporated, add the remaining flour mixture all at once, mixing on low speed to combine.

4. Pour the batter into the prepared pan and spread it evenly to the corners with a large offset spatula. Bake for 20 to 25 minutes, until the cake is golden brown and the top springs back when gently poked and a tester inserted into the center comes out clean.

5. While the cake bakes, line a work surface with a large sheet of parchment paper.

6. Set the sheet pan on a wire rack and let the cake cool for about 10 minutes, then run a paring knife around the edges to loosen the cake. Invert the cake onto the parchment-lined work surface, carefully remove the baked-on parchment, and allow to cool completely, about 15 minutes.

7. Meanwhile, in the bowl of a stand mixer fitted with the whisk attachment or in a large bowl with a handheld mixer, whip together the cream, confectioners' sugar, and crème fraîche on medium-high speed until medium-stiff peaks form, 3 to 5 minutes.

8. To make a rectangular two-layer cake, use a sharp knife to slice the cake in half crosswise. If you'd like, trim the outer edges of the cakes so that all of the sides are raw. Set one of the cake layers on a serving platter and spread with the jam, then top with the whipped cream (you can pipe the cream on top for a more polished look, or just spread it on in a thick, even layer). Gently place the second layer of cake on top. Refrigerate the cake, lightly covered, for at least 20 minutes (and up to a day).

9. Remove the cake from the refrigerator, dust the top lightly with confectioners' sugar, slice, and serve. The cake is best that day, but will keep, tightly wrapped, in the refrigerator for up to 3 days.

Maple Butternut Cake

SERVES 20

I feel like zucchini gets most of the glory in baking, but what about all the other squashes? As it turns out, butternut squash makes a deliciously intriguing addition to a simple spice cake, bringing welcome sweetness and moisture to the final bake. The spiced, squashy sponge pairs perfectly with a creamy maple frosting and makes a beautiful, delicate layer cake.

Cake

Nonstick cooking spray

2½ cups all-purpose flour

2 teaspoons baking powder

1 teaspoon baking soda

1½ teaspoons ground cardamom

½ teaspoon ground nutmeg

1 teaspoon kosher salt

4 large eggs

1½ cups granulated sugar

½ cup pure maple syrup

1¼ cups canola oil

1 tablespoon pure vanilla extract

3 cups shredded butternut squash

Frosting

¼ cup pure maple syrup

1 cup (2 sticks) unsalted butter, at room temperature

2 tablespoons brown sugar

4 cups confectioners' sugar

½ teaspoon kosher salt

2 tablespoons whole milk or heavy cream

1. MAKE THE CAKE: Preheat the oven to 350°F with a rack in the center position. Grease a sheet pan with nonstick spray, line it with parchment paper, and grease the parchment, too.

2. In a medium bowl, whisk the flour, baking powder, baking soda, cardamom, nutmeg, and salt.

3. In the bowl of a stand mixer fitted with the whisk attachment or in a large bowl with a handheld mixer, whip the eggs and granulated sugar together on high speed until light yellow and doubled in volume, about 5 minutes.

4. In a small bowl or large, spouted measuring cup, stir together the maple syrup, oil, and vanilla.

5. With the mixer running on medium speed, slowly pour the syrup mixture into the egg mixture and whip until incorporated, about 2 minutes. Add the dry ingredients and mix on low speed until just combined, then fold in the shredded squash with a rubber spatula.

6. Pour the batter into the prepared pan and spread it evenly to the corners with a large offset spatula. Bake for 25 to 30 minutes, until the cake is deeply golden brown and a tester inserted into the center comes out clean.

7. While the cake bakes, line a work surface with a large sheet of parchment paper.

8. Set the sheet pan on a wire rack and let the cake cool in the pan for about 10 minutes, then run a paring knife around the edges of the pan to loosen the cake. Invert the cake onto the parchment-lined work surface, carefully remove the baked-on parchment from the cake, and allow to cool completely, about 15 minutes.

recipe continues

9. MEANWHILE, MAKE THE FROSTING: In the bowl of a stand mixer fitted with the paddle attachment or in a large bowl with a handheld mixer, beat together the maple syrup, butter, brown sugar, confectioners' sugar, salt, and milk on medium-high speed until smooth and spreadable, 3 to 5 minutes.

10. To make a rectangular two-layer cake, use a sharp knife to slice the sheet cake in half crosswise. Set one half of the cake on a serving platter and spread with a generous layer of frosting, then place the second half of the cake carefully on top. Spread the rest of the frosting over the top of the cake, leaving the sides bare.

11. Slice and serve the cake immediately. The cake will keep, uncovered, in the refrigerator for up to 3 days.

How Do I: Cut Through a Tough Butternut Squash?

No matter how sharp your knife, cutting through a big, beautiful butternut squash can be a dangerous feat. So how can we do it safely and easily? First, use your sharp knife to score the squash around the outside, then simply microwave the whole squash for 3 to 5 minutes to soften slightly. Once cool, the squash will be much easier to cut in half at the neck—then just peel and grate (either with a box grater or in the food processor). Voilà! We've got squash for our cake *and* all of our fingers intact! Two good things, I think you'll agree.

Black Forest Swiss Roll

SERVES 8 TO 10

A spiral of chocolate sponge, thick cream swirled with tart cherry jam, and a rich blanket of dark chocolate ganache make this cake one of my absolute favorites. Don't stress if the cake cracks a little bit when unrolled—the cherry cream and ganache will patch it up and hide all sins. If you can't get your hands on cherry preserves, find some good raspberry jam for a delicious substitute.

Cake

- Nonstick cooking spray
- ⅔ cup all-purpose flour
- ⅓ cup plus ¼ cup unsweetened cocoa powder, plus more for dusting
- ½ teaspoon baking powder
- ½ teaspoon kosher salt
- 6 large eggs
- 1 cup granulated sugar
- ½ teaspoon pure vanilla extract
- ¼ cup vegetable oil
- ¼ cup strong brewed coffee
- ¼ cup confectioners' sugar

Filling

- 1 cup heavy cream, cold
- 8 ounces mascarpone cheese
- ¼ cup granulated sugar
- Kosher salt
- ¾ cup cherry preserves
- 1 to 2 tablespoons cherry liqueur, such as Luxardo (optional)

Ganache Topping

- 6 ounces semisweet or bittersweet chocolate, chopped, or chocolate chips
- ½ cup heavy cream

1. MAKE THE CAKE: Preheat the oven to 350°F with a rack in the center position. Grease a sheet pan with nonstick spray, line it with parchment paper, and grease the parchment, too.

2. Sift the flour, ⅓ cup of the cocoa powder, the baking powder, and salt into a medium bowl and whisk to combine.

3. In the bowl of a stand mixer fitted with the whisk attachment or in a large bowl with a handheld mixer, whip the eggs and granulated sugar together on high speed until pale yellow and thick, about 5 minutes. Mix in the vanilla, then slowly drizzle in the oil and coffee while the mixer continues to run. Turn off the mixer, then fold in the dry ingredients with a whisk until the batter is smooth and homogeneous.

4. Pour the batter into the prepared pan and spread it evenly to the corners with a large offset spatula. Bake for about 8 minutes, until the cake is just set and a tester inserted into the center comes out clean.

5. While the cake bakes, lay a clean dish towel on a work surface and fill a fine-mesh sieve with the confectioners' sugar and remaining ¼ cup cocoa powder.

6. Remove the cake from the oven and immediately run a paring knife around the edges of the pan to loosen the cake. Working quickly while the cake is still hot, sift a thin layer of the confectioners' sugar and cocoa mixture over the cake, then turn the cake out of the pan onto the dish towel, sugared side down. Carefully remove the baked-on parchment from the cake, then sprinkle a layer of confectioners' sugar and cocoa where the parchment used to be. Gently roll up the cake and the towel, starting from a short side and rolling away from yourself. Let the cake cool completely, about 25 minutes.

recipe continues

7. MEANWHILE, MAKE THE FILLING: In a large bowl, whisk together the cream, mascarpone, granulated sugar, and a pinch of salt until thick, smooth, and spreadable. Fold in the cherry preserves and cherry liqueur, if using.

8. Once the cake is cool, unroll it onto a work surface (it may crack a bit, but that's okay). Spread the cherry cream filling over the cake, leaving a ½-inch border. Tightly but gently roll up the cake with the filling inside (this time leave the towel behind). If you'd like, use a serrated knife to trim the ends of the roll to make neat edges. Carefully transfer the cake to a serving platter, seam side down.

9. MAKE THE GANACHE: Place the chopped chocolate in a medium heatproof bowl. Warm the cream in a small saucepan over medium heat until just bubbling around the edges, about 5 minutes. Pour the warm cream over the chocolate. Let sit for 3 minutes, then slowly whisk the chocolate and cream together until smooth and shiny. Let the ganache cool, stirring occasionally, until it's just warm, but no longer hot to the touch, about 7 minutes.

10. Pour the ganache over the cake. Slice and serve immediately. The cake will keep, tightly covered, in the refrigerator for up to 3 days.

Pumpkin Tiramisu Roll

SERVES 8 TO 10

She's pumpkin cake! She's tiramisu! She's pumpkin cake and tiramisu, all rolled up into one! Quite literally, I mean. The combination of pumpkin, coffee, warm spices, and cream is a surprising delight of flavors, and the pretty roulade, all dressed up with a bracing amount of cocoa powder on top, is ready for her close-up. And to be served with a hot cup of coffee.

Cake

Nonstick cooking spray
1 cup cake flour
1 teaspoon ground cinnamon
1 teaspoon ground ginger
¼ teaspoon ground nutmeg
¼ teaspoon ground allspice
⅛ teaspoon ground cloves
½ teaspoon baking soda
½ teaspoon kosher salt
5 large eggs
1 cup granulated sugar
1 cup canned pure pumpkin puree, such as Libby's
Confectioners' sugar

Filling

2 tablespoons instant espresso powder
8 ounces mascarpone cheese
1 cup heavy cream, cold
½ cup granulated sugar
2 tablespoons dark rum or pure vanilla extract
Kosher salt
2 tablespoons unsweetened cocoa powder

1. MAKE THE CAKE: Preheat the oven to 350°F with a rack in the center position. Grease a sheet pan with nonstick spray, line it with parchment paper, and grease the parchment, too.

2. Sift the flour, cinnamon, ginger, nutmeg, allspice, cloves, and baking soda into a medium bowl. Whisk in the salt until combined.

3. In the bowl of a stand mixer fitted with the whisk attachment or in a large bowl with a handheld mixer, whip the eggs and granulated sugar together on high speed until pale yellow and thick, about 5 minutes. Add the pumpkin puree and mix on low speed, just until combined. Add the flour mixture and mix on low speed again until no streaks remain.

4. Pour the batter into the prepared pan and spread it evenly to the corners with a large offset spatula. Bake 6 to 8 minutes, until the cake is just golden and springs back when lightly poked.

5. While the cake bakes, lay a clean dish towel on a work surface and fill a fine-mesh sieve with about ½ cup confectioners' sugar.

6. Remove the cake from the oven and immediately run a paring knife around the edges of the pan to loosen the cake. Working quickly while the cake is still hot, sift a thin layer of confectioners' sugar over the cake, then turn the cake out of the pan onto the dish towel, sugared side down. Carefully remove the baked-on parchment from the cake, then sprinkle a layer of confectioners' sugar where the parchment used to be. Gently roll up the cake and the towel, starting from a short side and rolling away from yourself. Let the cake cool completely in the towel, about 35 minutes.

7. MEANWHILE, MAKE THE FILLING: In the bowl of a stand mixer fitted with the whisk attachment or in a large bowl with a handheld mixer, whip together the espresso powder, mascarpone, cream, granulated sugar, rum, and a pinch of salt on medium-high speed until thick and creamy, 3 to 5 minutes.

8. When the cake is cool, unroll it onto a work surface. Spread the mascarpone cream over the cake, leaving a ½-inch border. Tightly but gently roll up the cake with the filling inside (this time leave the towel behind). If you'd like, use a serrated knife to trim the ends of the roll to make neat edges. Carefully transfer the cake to a serving platter, seam side down.

9. Sprinkle the top of the roulade with the cocoa powder, then cut the cake into thick slices to serve. The cake will keep, loosely covered, in the refrigerator for 2 to 3 days.

photograph follows

Mint Chocolate Chip Meringue Roll

SERVES 8 TO 10

I got the idea for this naturally gluten-free cake from Zoë François, a wonderful author, baker, and meringue whisperer extraordinaire. In her beautiful cookbook Zoë Bakes Cakes, *Zoë makes a pavlova roulade stuffed with stewed rhubarb and cream—the whole thing's an elegant, marshmallow-y dream. I wanted to play with the flavor combination but keep that crispy-edged, soft-and-dreamy interior texture, so here is my mint chocolate chip meringue roll. It's both whimsical and elegant, comfortable on the good china at a fancy gathering or on paper plates at a backyard BBQ. I hope you enjoy it as much as I do.*

Meringue

Nonstick cooking spray

5 large egg whites, at room temperature

Kosher salt

⅛ teaspoon cream of tartar

3 tablespoons cold water

1¼ cups granulated sugar

1 tablespoon plus 1 teaspoon cornstarch

1 teaspoon pure peppermint or mint extract

1 teaspoon apple cider vinegar

⅓ cup mini chocolate chips

Confectioners' sugar

Filling

2 cups heavy cream, cold

2 tablespoons confectioners' sugar

¼ teaspoon pure peppermint or mint extract

3 or 4 drops of green food coloring

⅓ cup mini chocolate chips

1. MAKE THE CAKE: Preheat the oven to 350°F with a rack in the center position. Grease a sheet pan with nonstick spray, line it with parchment paper, and grease the parchment, too.

2. In the bowl of a stand mixer fitted with the whisk attachment or in a large bowl with a handheld mixer, whip the egg whites, a pinch of salt, and the cream of tartar on medium-high speed until medium peaks form, about 3 minutes. With the mixer running, drizzle in the water, then very slowly add the granulated sugar. Once all of the sugar is incorporated, increase the mixer speed to high and whip until very stiff, glossy peaks form, about 5 minutes. Fold in the cornstarch, peppermint extract, and apple cider vinegar with a rubber spatula until incorporated, then fold in the chocolate chips until well distributed.

3. Transfer the meringue to the prepared pan and spread it evenly to the corners with a large offset spatula. Bake the meringue for 10 to 15 minutes, until puffy and just starting to brown. Dust the top of the meringue with confectioners' sugar, cover with a clean dish towel, and allow the meringue to cool completely in the pan, about 30 minutes.

4. MEANWHILE, MAKE THE FILLING: In the bowl of a stand mixer fitted with the whisk attachment or in a large bowl with a handheld mixer, whip the cream with the confectioners' sugar and peppermint extract on medium speed until medium peaks form, about 5 minutes. Fold in the green food coloring with a rubber spatula until your desired shade of green is reached.

recipe continues

5. ASSEMBLE THE ROLL: Place a sheet of parchment paper or a clean dish towel on a work surface and dust liberally with confectioners' sugar. Invert the meringue onto the parchment and carefully remove the baked-on parchment. Spread the whipped cream evenly and generously over the meringue, leaving a ½-inch border, then sprinkle with the chocolate chips. Roll up the meringue, starting from a short side and using the parchment to help, as tightly as possible. Carefully transfer the meringue roll to a serving platter, seam side down. Transfer the meringue roll, uncovered, to the refrigerator to rest for at least 1 hour or up to overnight (this will make for easier slicing).

6. Remove the meringue roll from the refrigerator and dust with confectioners' sugar before slicing and serving. Leftovers will keep, loosely covered, in the refrigerator for up to 2 days.

Tell Me: **What's the Difference Between Liquid and Gel Food Coloring?**

Both liquid and gel food coloring help us punch up the colors of batters, fillings, and buttercreams—but what's the difference between the two, and can we use them interchangeably? Traditional liquid food coloring is water-based, with a thin and (surprise, surprise) liquid viscosity. It's not as strong as gel food coloring, meaning you need to use more to achieve your desired color, and it often produces lighter, more pastel colors. Gel food coloring is thicker and more concentrated, producing brighter, stronger hues with just a small drop. They are generally interchangeable, so go ahead and use either liquid or gel—just remember that liquid food coloring produces paler colors, and gel coloring will give you a more vibrant hue.

Boston Cream Pie

SERVES 18 TO 20

I lived in Boston for a while after graduating college, and although being in your early twenties is a weird time and I think I've blocked a lot of it from memory, I can't say that I ever ran into a slice of Boston cream pie while in the city (unless you count the "Boston Kreme" option from Dunkin' Donuts, which honestly slaps, but I'm not sure counts as the real thing). The combination of tender vanilla cake ("pie" is a misnomer), thick vanilla custard, and glossy chocolate ganache is a true winner, though, and I wanted to give you a version that is as easy to make as it is to eat. Start with a quick vanilla sponge and use a secret pantry ingredient (Hint: rhymes with Yell-O) to make a faux (yet still wonderful) pastry cream in just minutes. The layered beauty that results is a truly craveable treat, in Boston and everywhere else, too.

Cake

Nonstick cooking spray

4 large eggs

1⅓ cups sugar

11 tablespoons unsalted butter, melted and cooled

1 cup whole milk

2 teaspoons pure vanilla extract

2 cups all-purpose flour

2 teaspoons baking powder

1 teaspoon kosher salt

Filling

1½ cups heavy cream, cold

¼ cup plus 2 tablespoons instant vanilla pudding mix, such as Jell-O

¼ cup plus 1 tablespoon whole milk

Ganache Topping

6 ounces semisweet or bittersweet chocolate, chopped, or chocolate chips

1½ teaspoons vegetable oil

Kosher salt

¼ cup plus 2 tablespoons heavy cream

1. MAKE THE CAKE: Preheat the oven to 325°F with a rack in the center position. Grease a sheet pan with nonstick spray, line it with parchment paper, and grease the parchment, too.

2. In the bowl of a stand mixer fitted with the whisk attachment or in a large bowl with a handheld mixer, whip together the eggs and sugar together on high speed until light yellow and doubled in volume, about 5 minutes. Add the melted butter, milk, and vanilla and mix on medium speed until combined. Add the flour, baking powder, and salt, and mix on low speed just until incorporated.

3. Pour the batter into the prepared pan and spread it evenly to the corners with a large offset spatula. Bake for about 12 minutes, until the cake is light brown and a tester inserted into the center comes out clean.

4. While the cake bakes, line a work surface with a large sheet of parchment paper.

5. Set the sheet pan on a wire rack and let the cake cool for 10 minutes, then run a paring knife around the edges of the pan to loosen the cake. Carefully invert it onto the parchment-lined surface, remove the baked-on parchment from the cake, and allow it to cool completely, about 25 minutes.

6. MEANWHILE, MAKE THE FILLING: In the bowl of a stand mixer fitted with the whisk attachment or in a large bowl with a handheld mixer, whip together the cream and pudding mix on medium-high speed until thick and smooth, about 3 minutes. With the mixer running on medium-low speed, slowly pour in the milk and mix until the cream is smooth and spreadable, 1 to 2 minutes.

7. Cut the cake in half crosswise and trim the outer edges of both pieces so that all of the sides are raw.

recipe continues

8. Place one layer of cake on a serving platter. Spread the vanilla cream in a thick, even layer over the cake, then carefully top with the remaining cake layer and press gently to adhere.

9. MAKE THE GANACHE TOPPING: Add the chopped chocolate, oil, and a pinch of salt to a heatproof medium bowl. In a small saucepan, warm the cream over medium heat until just bubbling around the edges, about 5 minutes. Pour the warm cream over the chocolate. Let sit for 3 minutes, then slowly whisk the chocolate and cream together until smooth and shiny.

10. Pour the ganache over the cake, spreading it to the corners and letting it drip gently over the sides in places. Transfer the Boston cream pie to the refrigerator, uncovered, for at least 30 minutes (and up to a day) to firm up.

11. Slice into pieces and serve. The cake will keep, well wrapped, in the refrigerator for 3 to 4 days.

Sunny Sprinkle Layer Cake

SERVES 8 TO 10

Both my children are of the mind that a treat isn't really a treat unless there are sprinkles involved. I get it. Sprinkles bring joy wherever they go, and a tender vanilla cake stuffed with the rainbow variety is bound to bring a smile to even the grumpiest grump (like a toddler whose carrots were sliced incorrectly, say, or a mother who only got a few hours of sleep). Whether meant to inspire happiness in kids or adults, served with cold milk or hot coffee, this cake is the sunniest way forward.

Cake

Nonstick cooking spray

3½ cups all-purpose flour

2 cups granulated sugar

2½ teaspoons baking soda

1½ teaspoons baking powder

1 teaspoon kosher salt

4 large eggs

4 tablespoons (½ stick) unsalted butter, melted and cooled

¼ cup canola oil

1¼ cups buttermilk

½ teaspoon pure almond extract

1 tablespoon pure vanilla extract

1 cup boiling water

½ cup rainbow sprinkles

Frosting

1 cup (2 sticks) unsalted butter, at room temperature

3½ cups confectioners' sugar

2 tablespoons whole milk

1 tablespoon pure vanilla extract

Rainbow sprinkles

1. MAKE THE CAKE: Preheat the oven to 350°F with a rack in the center position. Grease a sheet pan with nonstick spray, line it with parchment paper, and grease the parchment, too.

2. In a large bowl, whisk together the flour, granulated sugar, baking soda, baking powder, and salt until combined. Make a well in the center of the bowl, then add the eggs, melted butter, oil, buttermilk, almond extract, and vanilla and whisk until a thick batter comes together. Slowly whisk in the boiling water until the batter has thinned and become smooth. Stir in the sprinkles with a rubber spatula.

3. Pour the batter into the prepared pan and spread it evenly to the corners with a large offset spatula. Bake for 25 to 30 minutes, until the cake is golden brown and a tester inserted into the center comes out clean.

4. While the cake bakes, line a work surface with a large sheet of parchment paper.

5. Let the cake cool in the pan for 10 minutes, then run a paring knife around the edges of the pan to loosen the cake. Carefully invert it onto the parchment-lined surface, remove the baked-on parchment from the cake, and allow to cool completely, about 20 minutes.

6. MEANWHILE, MAKE THE FROSTING: In the bowl of a stand mixer fitted with the paddle attachment or in a large bowl with a handheld mixer, beat the butter on medium-high speed until fluffy, about 3 minutes, then add the confectioners' sugar, whole milk,

recipe continues

and vanilla and beat on high speed for 3 to 5 minutes, until smooth and bright white.

7. To make a round, three-layer cake, use the tip of a paring knife to cut out three 6¾-inch circles from the sheet cake (use an inverted bowl, plate, or cardboard round as a guide). Save any cake scraps to use for decorating.

8. Place one round cake layer on a serving platter and use an offset spatula to spread about 1 cup of the frosting over the top, all the way to the edges. Repeat with the remaining cake layers, using the offset spatula to spread a thin layer of frosting on the top and sides of the entire cake. Refrigerate the cake for about 10 minutes to firm up the crumb coat.

9. Meanwhile, cut the cake scraps into cubes or break them up into crumbs.

10. Spread the rest of the frosting in a thick layer over the top and sides of the cake. While the frosting is still sticky, arrange the cake cubes or crumbs on top of the cake and decorate with more sprinkles.

11. Let the cake firm up, uncovered, in the refrigerator for at least 20 minutes before slicing and serving. The cake will keep, loosely covered, in the refrigerator for up to 3 days.

Red Velvet Cake
with White Chocolate Frosting

SERVES 10 TO 12

A classic red velvet cake is soft and velvety in texture, faintly chocolaty in flavor, and typically paired with tangy cream cheese frosting. I like to make mine with a creamy white chocolate frosting, which is unexpectedly delicious and veers away from being cloyingly sweet with the addition of tangy sour cream. Using gel food coloring gives the strongest tint to the batter, but if all you have is liquid food coloring, that'll work just fine.

Cake

Nonstick cooking spray

4 large eggs

2½ cups granulated sugar

1½ cups buttermilk

1 cup vegetable oil

1 tablespoon pure vanilla extract

1 teaspoon kosher salt

1 teaspoon red gel food coloring

¼ cup unsweetened cocoa powder

3½ cups all-purpose flour

1 tablespoon baking powder

1 teaspoon baking soda

Frosting

1½ cups (3 sticks) unsalted butter, at room temperature

4½ cups confectioners' sugar

1 tablespoon pure vanilla extract

6 ounces white chocolate, melted

3 tablespoons sour cream

Kosher salt

1. MAKE THE CAKE: Preheat the oven to 350°F with a rack in the center position. Grease a sheet pan with nonstick spray, line it with parchment paper, and grease the parchment, too.

2. In a large bowl, vigorously whisk the eggs and granulated sugar until pale and frothy, 1 to 2 minutes. Whisk in the buttermilk, oil, vanilla, and salt until smooth. Whisk in the food coloring until combined. Sift the cocoa powder into the bowl, then add the flour, baking powder, and baking soda. Fold with the whisk until the batter is smooth and streak-free.

3. Pour the batter into the prepared pan and spread it evenly to the corners with a large offset spatula. Bake for about 15 minutes, until the cake is springy and a tester inserted into the center comes out clean.

4. While the cake bakes, line a work surface with a large sheet of parchment paper.

5. Let the cake cool in the pan for 15 minutes, then run a paring knife around the edges of the pan to loosen the cake. Carefully invert it onto the parchment-lined surface, remove the baked-on parchment from the cake, and allow to cool completely, 15 to 20 minutes.

6. MEANWHILE, MAKE THE FROSTING: In the bowl of a stand mixer fitted with the paddle attachment or in a large bowl with a handheld mixer, beat the butter on medium-high speed until fluffy, 3 to 5 minutes, then add the confectioners' sugar, vanilla, melted white chocolate, sour cream, and a pinch of salt and beat on high speed for 3 to 5 minutes, until smooth and fluffy.

recipe continues

7. To make a four-layer rectangular cake, use a sharp knife to cut the sheet cake in half lengthwise, then again crosswise. Place one rectangular cake layer on a serving platter and use an offset spatula to spread a thin layer of frosting over the top, all the way to the edges. Repeat with the remaining cake layers (if you prefer a three-layer cake, cut the fourth layer into cubes or break into crumbs to use for decorating). Use the offset spatula to spread a thin layer of frosting over the top and sides of the entire cake. Refrigerate the cake for about 10 minutes to firm up the crumb coat.

8. Spread the rest of the frosting in a thick layer over the top and sides of the cake. While the frosting is still sticky, arrange any reserved cake cubes or crumbs on top of the cake.

9. Slice and serve immediately. The cake will keep, loosely covered, in the refrigerator for up to 3 days.

Lemon Poppy Seed Layer Cake

SERVES 8 TO 10

There's something so playful about the pairing of lemon and poppy seeds. The lemon brings a bright, zingy flavor, and the poppy seeds bring that delicate, crunchy pop—you know they're having a great time together, singing karaoke and pouring each other tall glasses of champagne. The addition of a perky lemon cream cheese frosting only enhances this party, so I suggest you make this cake and join the fun.

Cake

Nonstick cooking spray

1¾ cups granulated sugar

Zest of 2 lemons

1 cup whole milk

½ cup fresh lemon juice

3 cups all-purpose flour

1½ teaspoons baking powder

½ teaspoon baking soda

½ teaspoon kosher salt

½ cup plus 2 tablespoons (1¼ sticks) unsalted butter, at room temperature

5 large eggs

½ cup vegetable oil

½ teaspoon pure vanilla extract

2 tablespoons poppy seeds

Frosting

1 (8-ounce) package cream cheese, at room temperature

1 cup (2 sticks) unsalted butter, at room temperature

4 cups confectioners' sugar

½ teaspoon pure vanilla extract

Zest of 1 lemon

Kosher salt

1. MAKE THE CAKE: Preheat the oven to 350°F with a rack in the center position. Grease a sheet pan with nonstick spray, line it with parchment paper, and grease the parchment, too.

2. In the bowl of a stand mixer fitted with the paddle attachment or in a large bowl with a handheld mixer, mix the granulated sugar and lemon zest together on low speed until the sugar turns yellow and fragrant, 3 to 5 minutes.

3. Meanwhile, combine the milk and lemon juice in a large, spouted measuring cup.

4. In a medium bowl, whisk together the flour, baking powder, baking soda, and salt.

5. Add the butter to the lemon sugar, increase the mixer speed to medium-high, and cream the butter and sugar together until light and fluffy, 3 to 5 minutes. Add the eggs one at a time, beating well and scraping down the sides of the bowl after each addition. With the mixer running on medium speed, slowly drizzle in the oil and vanilla until well combined.

6. Reduce the mixer speed to low and alternate adding the dry ingredients and the milk mixture, beginning and ending with the dry ingredients. Mix until just combined. Fold in the poppy seeds with a rubber spatula until evenly distributed.

7. Pour the batter into the prepared pan and spread it evenly to the corners with a large offset spatula. Bake for 25 to 30 minutes, until the cake is golden brown and a tester inserted into the center comes out clean.

recipe continues

8. While the cake bakes, line a work surface with a large sheet of parchment paper.

9. Set the sheet pan on a wire rack and let the cake cool for about 10 minutes, then run a paring knife around the edges to loosen the cake. Carefully invert it onto the parchment-lined work surface, remove the baked-on parchment from the cake, and allow it to cool completely, about 20 minutes.

10. MEANWHILE, MAKE THE FROSTING: In the bowl of a stand mixer fitted with the paddle attachment or in a large bowl with a handheld mixer, beat the cream cheese and butter together on medium-high speed until smooth and fluffy, 3 to 5 minutes. Add the confectioners' sugar, vanilla, lemon zest, and a pinch of salt and beat on high speed until creamy and light, about 5 minutes.

11. To make a round, three-layer cake, use the tip of a paring knife to cut out three 6¾-inch circles from the sheet cake (use an inverted bowl, plate, or cardboard round as a guide). Save any cake scraps to use for decorating.

12. Place one round cake layer on a serving platter and use an offset spatula to spread about 1 cup of the frosting over the top, all the way to the edges. Repeat with the remaining cake layers, using the offset spatula to spread a thin layer of frosting over the top and sides of the entire cake. Refrigerate the cake for about 10 minutes to firm up the crumb coat.

13. Meanwhile, cut the cake scraps into cubes or break them up into crumbs.

14. Spread the rest of the frosting in a thick layer over the top and sides of the cake. While the frosting is still sticky, arrange the cake cubes or crumbs on top of the cake.

15. Slice and serve immediately. The cake will keep, loosely covered, in the refrigerator for up to 3 days.

Bars

Squares to Share

There's just something so wholesome about bar cookies. They're not here to make trouble. There's an innately friendly, potluck-y, vaguely Midwestern, warm, and cozy vibe about the bar cookie, and given how hard it can feel to just be a person in the world, I think it's safe to say we're all here for it.

A good bar is easy to throw together, easy to transport, and, best of all, easy to eat! And bar cookies baked on a sheet pan means *plenty* of bars to share. Whether we're stocking up the school bake sale, impressing at the office, or punching up the neighborhood block party, I've covered the basics with everything from Swirled Brownie Cheesecake Bars (page 121), Toasted S'more Blondies (page 104), and Berry Shortbread Crumble Bars (page 108), to the beyond with Butter Mochi Squares (page 112) and Cherry Almond Clafoutis Squares (page 103). Take your pick, pour yourself a hot cup of coffee or tea, and put your feet up—bar cookies are our new version of self-care.

Salty Sweet Brown Sugar Cookie Bars

MAKES 24 BARS

It may seem counterintuitive, but adding salt really brings out the sweetness in baked goods, and I love the play between sweet and salty in these simple but dressed-up blondies. Using brown sugar amps up the deep, toasty caramel notes, and the addition of pretzels, pecans, flaky sea salt, and an extra caramel drizzle really takes the cake. Or the cookie bar. You get it.

Nonstick cooking spray

3¼ cups all-purpose flour

1 tablespoon baking powder

1 teaspoon kosher salt

1½ cups (3 sticks) unsalted butter, at room temperature

2¾ cups packed dark brown sugar

3 large eggs

1 tablespoon pure vanilla extract

2 cups small pretzel twists

1 cup pecans, roughly chopped (optional)

1 cup caramel sauce, homemade (see below) or store-bought, warmed

Flaky sea salt, such as Maldon

1. Preheat the oven to 350°F with a rack in the center position. Grease a sheet pan with nonstick spray.

2. In a medium bowl, whisk together the flour, baking powder, and kosher salt.

3. In the bowl of a stand mixer fitted with the paddle attachment or in a large bowl with a handheld mixer, cream together the butter and brown sugar on medium-high speed until fluffy and combined, about 3 minutes. Add the eggs one at a time, beating well and scraping down the sides of the bowl after each addition. Mix in the vanilla. Add the dry ingredients and mix on low speed until the dough just comes together.

4. Transfer the dough to the prepared pan and use a greased hand to press it evenly to the corners. Gently smooth the top with an offset spatula. Crumble the pretzels and scatter the pecans over the dough, pressing in gently to adhere. Bake the bars for 12 to 16 minutes, until lightly browned and a tester inserted into the center comes out clean. Allow the bars to cool completely in the pan, about 30 minutes.

5. Drizzle the caramel sauce over the bars, then sprinkle with flaky sea salt. Cut into pieces. The bars will keep, tightly covered, in the refrigerator for up to a week.

Make It Yourself: Caramel Sauce

For a quick and easy homemade caramel sauce, combine 1½ cups sugar and ½ cup water in a large saucepan over medium heat. Once the sugar has dissolved, increase the heat and boil, without stirring, until the mixture turns a deep amber color, swirling the pan occasionally to evenly distribute heat. Once the sugar reaches stage amber, quickly remove the pan from the heat and whisk in 3 tablespoons unsalted butter until smooth and incorporated. (Caution: The mixture will hiss and bubble up once you add the butter—keep your face and fingers away from the pot.) Whisk in 1 cup heavy cream and 1 teaspoon flaky sea salt, then carefully pour the hot caramel into a glass jar and let it cool to room temperature before using. The caramel will keep, tightly covered, in the refrigerator for up to 2 weeks!

Cherry Almond Clafoutis Squares

MAKES 24 BARS

I first tried cherry clafoutis while studying abroad in France, and I'm still proud of myself for ordering it, despite not knowing anything about it or even how to correctly pronounce it (FYI: Kla-FOO-tee). Turns out, clafoutis is a classic French country dessert of fresh fruit (usually cherries) combined with a sweet, eggy batter that when baked, to me lives somewhere between a custard and a pancake—somehow soft, silky, and solid all at once. These cherry almond squares are clafoutis in bar form, with a sweet, nutty crust to hold up the softer baked fruit layer. Either fresh or frozen cherries work well here, though if you go with frozen, do not thaw them before scattering over the crust. If you can't find cherries at all, fresh raspberries make a lovely substitute.

Crust

Nonstick cooking spray

7 ounces almond paste

⅓ cup granulated sugar

1 teaspoon pure vanilla extract

¾ teaspoon kosher salt

1 cup (2 sticks) unsalted butter, melted

2 cups all-purpose flour

Clafoutis Layer

5 large eggs

1 cup granulated sugar

1 teaspoon pure vanilla extract

¼ teaspoon pure almond extract

½ teaspoon kosher salt

¾ cup all-purpose flour

1 cup (2 sticks) unsalted butter, melted

2 pounds fresh or frozen (not thawed) pitted cherries (I like a mix of sweet and tart)

Confectioners' sugar

1. MAKE THE CRUST: Preheat the oven to 375°F with a rack in the center position. Grease a sheet pan with nonstick spray.

2. In the bowl of a stand mixer fitted with the paddle attachment or in a large bowl with a handheld mixer, beat together the almond paste, granulated sugar, vanilla, and salt on medium-high speed until crumbly and combined, 3 to 5 minutes. Add the melted butter and beat until smooth, about 2 minutes. Add the flour and mix on low speed until the dough just comes together, 1 minute more.

3. Press the dough into the bottom of the prepared pan (it will look scant, but keep pushing it out until it fills the pan evenly). Bake for 13 to 15 minutes, until the crust is just golden. Allow to cool for 5 to 10 minutes.

4. MEANWHILE, MAKE THE CLAFOUTIS LAYER: In a large bowl, whisk the together the eggs, granulated sugar, vanilla, almond extract, and salt. With a rubber spatula, stir in the flour, then the melted butter, until smooth.

5. Arrange the cherries over the crust, spacing them evenly, then carefully pour the clafoutis filling evenly over the cherries. Bake the bars for 35 to 40 minutes, until golden brown and set. Allow the bars to cool completely in the pan, about 30 minutes. Dust lightly with confectioners' sugar.

6. Slice into pieces. The bars will keep, tightly covered, in the refrigerator for up to 4 days.

Toasted S'more Blondies

MAKES 20 TO
25 BLONDIES

We love a blondie! Especially one that's all dressed up for summer camp. Studded with dark chocolate and graham cracker pieces and topped with toasty marshmallows, these bars are ready for buddy check at the lake, and also to walk awkwardly behind the cute boy from bunk 5 on the way to play capture the flag. The nice thing is that although these s'more-flavored treats evoke summertime fun, they can be made and enjoyed any time of year, no campfire needed.

Nonstick cooking spray

3 cups all-purpose flour

2 teaspoons baking powder

1 teaspoon kosher salt

1½ cups (3 sticks) unsalted butter

2 cups packed dark brown sugar

1 cup granulated sugar

4 large eggs

1 tablespoon pure vanilla extract

1½ cups bittersweet chocolate chips

6 whole graham crackers, broken into small pieces

12 ounces mini marshmallows

1. Preheat the oven to 350°F with a rack in the center position. Grease a sheet pan with nonstick spray.

2. In a large bowl, whisk together the flour, baking powder, and salt.

3. Melt the butter in a medium pot over medium heat. Cook, stirring often, until the butter turns a toasted, amber color (it will bubble and spit; when it quiets down, check for browning). Pour the browned butter into a large heatproof bowl, making sure to scrape the pot for all those delicious browned bits, then whisk in the brown sugar and granulated sugar until well combined (the mixture may look grainy). Add the eggs one at a time, whisking well after each addition, then stir in the vanilla until smooth.

4. Gently stir the dry ingredients into the wet ingredients with a rubber spatula until a smooth dough just comes together. Fold in the chocolate chips and graham cracker pieces.

5. Transfer the dough to the prepared pan and spread it evenly to the corners with a large offset spatula. Bake the blondies for 18 minutes, until starting to set but still a bit soft and gooey. Remove the pan from the oven and scatter the marshmallows on top of the blondies, pressing gently to adhere. Return the pan to the oven and bake until the bars are set (a tester inserted into the center will come out mostly clean) and the marshmallows are nicely golden, about 12 minutes more. To really brown the marshmallows, set the pan under the broiler for about 30 seconds. Allow the bars to cool in the pan for 15 minutes.

6. Spray a large knife with nonstick spray, then slice the blondies into pieces. The bars are best the day they are made but will keep, tightly covered, at room temperature for 3 to 4 days.

Chocolate Mousse Squares

MAKES 24 TO 30
SQUARES

I remember growing up and hearing my grandparents, recently back from a special visit to Paris, talking about a fabulous delicacy they had discovered on their trip: "chocolate moose." Although seven-year-old me was disappointed to learn that chocolate mousse is not actually an animal/chocolate hybrid, grown-up me is happy to eat this airy custard, lightened with whipped cream, on any occasion. These rich and creamy bars come together without any fussing over raw eggs or yolks, which are traditionally used to make chocolate mousse; instead, the secret to fluffy, smooth, and sliceable chocolate mousse bars is store-bought marshmallows. Untraditional? Yes. Simple and delicious? Also yes.

Nonstick cooking spray

1 (14-ounce) box chocolate sandwich cookies (I like Oreos)

¾ cup (1½ sticks) unsalted butter, melted

2 teaspoons kosher salt

4 tablespoons (½ stick) unsalted butter

3 cups bittersweet chocolate chips

4 cups mini marshmallows

⅔ cup whole milk

1 tablespoon pure vanilla extract

4 cups heavy cream, cold

2 tablespoons sugar

Chocolate shavings (optional)

1. Preheat the oven to 350°F with a rack in the center position. Grease a sheet pan with nonstick spray.

2. In a food processor, pulse the chocolate sandwich cookies with the melted butter and 1 teaspoon of the salt until the cookies are finely ground and the texture resembles wet sand.

3. Press the cookie crust evenly against the bottom of the prepared pan. Bake the crust for 10 minutes, until just set. Allow to cool completely, about 15 minutes.

4. Meanwhile, in a large saucepan over medium heat, melt together the butter, chocolate chips, marshmallows, milk, and remaining 1 teaspoon salt until smooth and homogeneous, about 10 minutes. (Alternatively, melt in a large microwave-safe bowl in 30-second intervals in the microwave, stirring between, about 3 minutes total.) Stir in the vanilla, then allow to cool to room temperature, about 20 minutes.

5. In the bowl of a stand mixer fitted with the whisk attachment or in a large bowl with a handheld mixer, whip 3 cups of the cream on medium-high speed until stiff peaks form, about 5 minutes.

6. Fold the whipped cream into the cooled chocolate mixture until well combined, then pour the chocolate mousse over the crust and gently spread it evenly to the corners with a large offset spatula. Chill, uncovered, in the refrigerator for at least 1 hour or up to 1 day.

7. Just before serving, in the bowl of a stand mixer fitted with the whisk attachment or in a large bowl with a handheld mixer, whip the remaining 1 cup cream with the sugar on medium-high speed until medium-stiff peaks form, 3 to 5 minutes.

8. Pipe or spread the whipped cream on top of the mousse bars. Top with a few chocolate shavings, if desired. Slice into pieces. The bars will keep, without the whipped cream on top, tightly covered, in the refrigerator for 4 to 5 days. With the whipped cream, the bars will keep for 1 to 2 days.

Berry Shortbread Crumble Bars

MAKES 24 BARS

These sweet, tart, berry-studded bars lie somewhere between cookie and pie, which honestly feels like a really good place to be. They're tender, juicy, and portable, equally happy to be tucked into a school lunch box, paraded out for a quick dessert, or grabbed for a sweet breakfast on the go.

Nonstick cooking spray

2 cups sugar

1½ teaspoons baking powder

4 cups all-purpose flour

¾ teaspoon kosher salt

Zest of 1 lemon

1½ cups (3 sticks) unsalted butter, cut into cubes and chilled

2 large eggs

6 cups fresh mixed berries, such as blueberries, raspberries, and/or blackberries

1 tablespoon plus 1 teaspoon cornstarch

Juice of 1 lemon

1 teaspoon pure vanilla extract

1. Preheat the oven to 375°F with a rack in the center position. Grease a sheet pan with nonstick spray.

2. In a food processor, pulse together 1½ cups of the sugar, the baking powder, flour, and salt to combine. Add the lemon zest, butter, and eggs and process until a crumbly dough forms, about 1 minute. (Alternatively, bring the dough together in a large bowl with a pastry blender or fork.)

3. Pat three-quarters of the dough into the bottom of the prepared pan, pressing firmly into an even layer.

4. In a large bowl, toss the berries with the remaining ½ cup sugar, the cornstarch, lemon juice, and vanilla.

5. Spread the fruit in a single layer over the crust. Crumble the remaining dough evenly over the berries. Bake the bars for about 25 minutes, until the dough is golden and the berries are bubbling. Allow the bars to cool completely in the pan, about 30 minutes.

6. Slice into pieces. The bars will keep, tightly covered, in the refrigerator for up to 5 days.

Pumpkin Pie Bars

MAKES 24 BARS

Thanksgiving is one of my favorite holidays. We usually spend it with my large, loud family in Philadelphia, and it's always a large, loud, wine-forward affair. In our house, no Thanksgiving feast is complete without pumpkin pie. This version, in bar form, boasts a perfectly smooth and creamy pumpkin custard anchored by a simple graham cracker and pecan press-in crust. Topped with a spoonful of freshly whipped cream (see page 122, step 6), these pumpkin pie bars are fun to make and eat, and are guaranteed to feed a (large, loud, potentially overserved) crowd. One note: I do strongly recommend using Libby's pumpkin puree here. While there are lots of brands on the market, sometimes the classic gets the job done best.

Graham Cracker Crust

Nonstick cooking spray

3 cups graham cracker crumbs (from about 24 whole crackers)

1 heaping cup whole pecans or skinned hazelnuts

½ cup packed brown sugar

½ cup granulated sugar

½ cup (1 stick) unsalted butter, melted and cooled

½ teaspoon kosher salt

Pumpkin Filling

2 (15-ounce) cans pure pumpkin puree, preferably Libby's

1¼ cups granulated sugar

1 teaspoon kosher salt

2 heaping teaspoons ground cinnamon

1 teaspoon ground ginger

½ teaspoon ground cloves

½ teaspoon ground nutmeg

6 large eggs

1 cup whole milk

1½ cups heavy cream

Whipped cream, for serving (see page 122, step 6; optional)

1. Preheat the oven to 400°F with a rack in the center position. Grease a sheet pan with nonstick spray.

2. MAKE THE GRAHAM CRACKER CRUST: In a food processor, grind together the graham cracker crumbs and nuts until coarsely ground and well combined. Add the brown sugar, granulated sugar, melted butter, and salt and pulse to combine until the mixture resembles wet sand.

3. Pour the graham mixture evenly into the prepared pan and use your hands or a flat-bottomed measuring cup to press the crumbs firmly against the bottom and up the sides of the pan, making sure there are no holes or extra-thin spots anywhere.

4. MAKE THE PUMPKIN FILLING: In a large bowl, whisk together the pumpkin puree, granulated sugar, salt, cinnamon, ginger, cloves, and nutmeg until smooth. Whisk in the eggs until smooth, then add the milk and cream and whisk until homogeneous.

5. Pour the pumpkin custard over the prepared crust and very carefully transfer the pan to the oven. Bake the bars for 15 minutes, then reduce the oven temperature to 350°F and bake for 10 to 15 minutes more, until the custard is mostly set—the center should just barely jiggle. Allow the pumpkin bars to cool in the pan for 20 minutes before transferring to the refrigerator, uncovered, to cool completely, at least 30 minutes and up to overnight.

6. Slice the pumpkin bars into pieces and serve topped with a generous dollop of whipped cream, if desired. The bars will keep, tightly covered, in the refrigerator for up to a week.

Butter Mochi Squares

MAKES 24 TO 30 BARS

Made with sweet rice flour, eggs, and your choice of milk, butter mochi is a sweet, naturally gluten-free, cake-meets-custard treat hailing from Hawaii, where it's as popular on the potluck table as brownies or chocolate chip cookies are on the mainland. I love its soft, sticky, bouncy chew and sweet, faintly nutty vanilla flavor. It's highly adaptable as far as the milk you use—any mixture of coconut, evaporated, whole, and/or 2% works nicely. If you love coconut, it takes well to a sprinkling of coconut flakes on top, but is also perfectly lovely plain, eaten straight from the pan or the fridge. Sweet rice flour, also called mochiko, can be found at many well-stocked grocery stores, but if you have any trouble finding it locally, you can easily order it online.

Nonstick cooking spray

6 large eggs

2½ cups sugar

2 (13-ounce) cans unsweetened full-fat coconut milk

1 cup whole milk

2 tablespoons pure vanilla extract

3¾ cups sweet rice flour (mochiko), such as Blue Star

2½ teaspoons baking powder

1 teaspoon kosher salt

½ cup (1 stick) unsalted butter, melted and cooled

½ cup unsweetened coconut flakes, toasted (see headnote, page 33; optional)

1. Preheat the oven to 350°F with a rack in the center position. Grease a sheet pan with nonstick spray, line it with parchment paper, and grease the parchment, too.

2. In a large bowl, vigorously whisk together the eggs and sugar until pale yellow, 1 to 2 minutes. Whisk in the coconut milk, whole milk, and vanilla until smooth. Add the sweet rice flour, baking powder, and salt and whisk until well combined, then whisk in the melted butter until smooth.

3. Pour the batter into the prepared pan and spread it evenly to the corners with a rubber spatula (it will seem like way too much batter, but don't worry) and sprinkle the toasted coconut, if using, on top. Bake for 30 to 35 minutes, until the butter mochi is crackled and golden and bounces back when lightly poked. Allow to cool completely in the pan, about 25 minutes.

4. Slice into pieces. The butter mochi will keep, tightly covered, at room temperature or in the refrigerator for up to 4 days.

Patchwork Cookie Bars

MAKES 20 TO 25 BARS

One of the benefits of working with a whole sheet pan is that, if we're feeling so inclined, we can make multiple different kinds of cookie bars in just one pan. In fact, this recipe makes multiple kinds of cookie dough from just one batter! Start with a simple cookie dough, then split it up and flavor it three ways: double chocolate chip, oatmeal cranberry, and coconut chip. After spreading all three batters out in the pan and baking up the bars, we're left with a warm patchwork quilt of bar cookies, and the proud feeling that we've got a little something sweet for everyone.

Nonstick cooking spray

1 cup (2 sticks) unsalted butter, at room temperature

1 cup granulated sugar

1 cup packed brown sugar

3 large eggs

1 tablespoon pure vanilla extract

2 cups all-purpose flour

1 teaspoon baking soda

1 teaspoon baking powder

1 teaspoon kosher salt

¼ cup unsweetened cocoa powder

½ cup white chocolate chips

½ cup candy-coated chocolates (I like M&M's)

1 cup rolled oats

1 teaspoon ground cinnamon

½ cup dried cranberries

½ cup chopped semisweet chocolate or chocolate chips

1 cup sweetened shredded coconut, toasted (see headnote, page 33)

1. Preheat the oven to 350°F with a rack in the center position. Grease a sheet pan with nonstick spray.

2. MAKE THE BASE DOUGH: In the bowl of a stand mixer fitted with the paddle attachment or in a large bowl with a handheld mixer, cream together the butter, granulated sugar, and brown sugar on medium-high speed until fluffy and combined, about 3 minutes. Add the eggs one at a time, beating well and scraping down the sides of the bowl after each addition, then mix in the vanilla. Add the flour, baking soda, baking powder, and salt and mix on low speed until just combined. Divide the dough evenly between three medium bowls (you can leave one-third in the mixing bowl).

3. In the first bowl, mix in the cocoa powder with a rubber spatula until smooth, then fold in the white chocolate chips and M&M's— this is the double chocolate chip dough. In the second bowl, fold in the oats, cinnamon, and cranberries—this is the oatmeal cookie dough. In the third bowl, fold in the chopped chocolate and toasted coconut—this is the chocolate coconut dough.

4. Divide each flavor of dough into three portions. Place the dough portions on the prepared pan, alternating in a "patchwork" pattern (alternatively, arrange the dough in three strips across the pan if you prefer to keep the flavors separate). Press and spread the dough out in an even layer to cover the pan completely (it will look scant, but will rise and expand in the oven). Bake for 20 to 25 minutes, until the cookie bars are well browned and a tester inserted into the center comes out with a few moist crumbs attached. Let the bars cool completely in the pan, about 35 minutes.

5. Slice into pieces, either keeping the flavors separate or mixing them together. The bars will keep, tightly covered, at room temperature for up to a week.

Buckeye Bars

MAKES 30 TO 50 BARS

Traditionally, buckeyes are sweet peanut butter candy balls dipped in chocolate, meant to look like the seeds of the buckeye tree, which is indigenous to Ohio. I've heard that Ohioans are quite protective of their buckeyes (the candy, not the tree, although hopefully both, because climate change), so I hope I don't offend anyone by adapting the lovely buckeye into these (very rich, meant to be sliced thinly) buckeye-flavored bars. There's a buttery, chocolate-cookie-crumb crust, a sweet peanut butter layer, and a mop of salted dark chocolate to finish. I think we can all agree that the combination of peanut butter and chocolate needs absolutely no improvement—10/10, no notes, sheer perfection. Well played, Ohio.

Nonstick cooking spray

1 (14-ounce) box chocolate sandwich cookies (I like Oreos), crumbled

¾ cup (1½ sticks) unsalted butter, melted

1½ teaspoons kosher salt

1¼ cups (2½ sticks) unsalted butter, at room temperature

2½ cups creamy peanut butter

1½ tablespoons pure vanilla extract

6¼ cups confectioners' sugar

1½ cups semisweet or bittersweet chocolate chips

1½ tablespoons coconut oil

Flaky sea salt, such as Maldon

1. Preheat the oven to 350°F with a rack in the center position. Grease a sheet pan with nonstick spray.

2. In a food processor, pulse together the cookie crumbs, melted butter, and 1 teaspoon of the kosher salt until the texture resembles wet sand.

3. Press the crumbs evenly against the bottom of the prepared pan, all the way to the corners. Bake the crust for 8 to 10 minutes, until just set and fragrant. Allow to cool completely, about 15 minutes.

4. In the bowl of a stand mixer fitted with the paddle attachment or in a large bowl with a handheld mixer, beat the room temperature butter with the peanut butter on medium-high speed until smooth and fluffy, 3 to 5 minutes. Add the vanilla, remaining ½ teaspoon kosher salt, and confectioners' sugar and mix on low speed until smooth and incorporated. Dollop the peanut butter mixture evenly over the cooled crust and gently spread in an even layer with a large offset spatula.

5. In a medium microwave-safe bowl, melt the chocolate chips and coconut oil together by microwaving in 30-second increments, stirring gently with a rubber spatula between, until smooth, about 2 minutes. (Alternatively, melt in a small saucepan over medium-low heat, about 5 minutes.)

6. Pour the melted chocolate mixture over the peanut butter layer in the pan and gently spread to the corners of the pan with a small offset spatula. Sprinkle the top generously with flaky sea salt.

7. Let the bars firm up, either at room temperature for about 30 minutes, or in the refrigerator, about 10 minutes.

8. Use a hot knife to cleanly slice into pieces. The bars will keep, tightly covered, in the refrigerator for up to a week.

Almond Frangipane Bars

MAKES 24 TO 30 BARS

Frangipane might sound fancy and intimidating—it's the filling used in desserts called pithivier and galette des rois, after all—but it's just a simple almond cream, easily blended together in the food processor. In fact, both the cookie base and the frangipane layer of these sweet, slightly floral almond bars are made in the food processor, so it turns out they're a snap to both make and eat. These sophisticated bars are a welcome afternoon treat with a cup of coffee or tea, and also make a sweet addition to a holiday cookie tin.

Cookie Base

Nonstick cooking spray

1½ cups (3 sticks) unsalted butter, cut into cubes and chilled

1½ cups granulated sugar

1½ teaspoons baking powder

3½ cups all-purpose flour

¾ teaspoon kosher salt

Zest of 1 orange

2 large eggs

Frangipane Topping

1 cup roasted almonds

⅓ cup unsalted butter, at room temperature

½ cup granulated sugar

1 large egg

½ teaspoon pure vanilla extract

1 tablespoon apricot jam

1 heaping cup sliced almonds

Confectioners' sugar

1. Preheat the oven to 375°F with a rack in the center position. Grease a sheet pan with nonstick spray.

2. MAKE THE COOKIE BASE: In a food processor, pulse together the butter, granulated sugar, baking powder, flour, salt, orange zest, and eggs until crumbly and combined, about 30 seconds.

3. Use your hands or a flat-bottomed measuring cup to press the crumbs firmly and evenly into the prepared pan, all the way to the corners.

4. MAKE THE FRANGIPANE TOPPING: In the food processor (no need to clean it out), pulse the roasted almonds until coarsely ground, about 1 minute. Add the butter, granulated sugar, egg, vanilla, and apricot jam and pulse until well combined and smooth, 1 to 2 minutes. Spread the frangipane topping evenly over the cookie base with a large offset spatula, making sure to reach the corners, then scatter the sliced almonds on top. Bake the bars for 10 to 12 minutes, until golden brown and slightly puffed. Allow the bars to cool completely in the pan, about 30 minutes.

5. Dust with confectioners' sugar, then slice into pieces. The bars will keep, tightly covered, at room temperature for up to 5 days.

All-the-Cereal Treats

MAKES 20 TO 30 BARS

I love a good crispy rice cereal treat—honestly, who doesn't? To me, what sets a good crispy rice treat apart from a great one is a soft and gooey texture, a deep and slightly nutty flavor (from browning the butter; I learned this trick from Deb Perelman of Smitten Kitchen*, a true American gem), and a good hit of salt to balance out the sweetness. The really good news is that we can make great crispy cereal treats entirely on a sheet pan! Yes, everything from browning the butter to melting the marshmallows to mixing up the treats can be done right on the pan, no extra bowls needed. Although you can choose pretty much any cereal you'd like here, I prefer cereals that are smaller in size (crisped rice, O's, or thin flakes, for example, instead of thicker puffs), as they seem to be easiest to incorporate and keep their crunch longer than others.*

¾ cup (1½ sticks) unsalted butter, cut into tablespoon-size chunks

20 ounces mini marshmallows

1 teaspoon pure vanilla extract

9 cups mixed cereal (I like a combination of Rice Krispies and Cocoa Pebbles)

½ teaspoon kosher salt

Flaky sea salt, such as Maldon

1. Preheat the oven to 375°F with a rack in the center position.

2. Place the butter on a sheet pan and warm it in the oven for about 5 minutes, until fully melted and just beginning to brown.

3. Remove the pan from the oven and carefully tilt from side to side to make sure the butter has coated the pan completely. Place the pan on a heatproof work surface and carefully add about three-quarters of the marshmallows, spreading them evenly on the pan. Return the pan to the oven and bake until the marshmallows have melted and are starting to brown, 3 to 5 minutes.

4. Return the pan to a work surface and add the vanilla, cereal, the rest of the marshmallows, and the kosher salt and carefully toss everything together with two rubber spatulas until well combined. Gently press the cereal treat mixture evenly into the pan, all the way to the corners, then sprinkle generously with flaky sea salt. Allow to cool slightly in the pan, about 10 minutes.

5. Slice into pieces. The treats can be served immediately (they're delicious while still slightly warm), or will keep, tightly covered, at room temperature for up to a week.

Swirled Brownie Cheesecake Bars

MAKES 24 BARS

My first book, Sheet Pan Suppers, includes a recipe for "thinnest brownies" that's proven to be a sleeper hit. Short in stature but chewy and fudgy in texture and flavor, I still get comments from people who claim to love them above all other brownies. This recipe is a riff on those beloved brownies, with a soft and sweet cream cheese swirl and a tumble of tiny chocolate chips for crunch. Dare I say they're even better than the original?

Brownie Layer

Nonstick cooking spray

1½ cups (3 sticks) unsalted butter

2 cups bittersweet chocolate chips

6 large eggs

2 cups sugar

1 teaspoon pure vanilla extract

1 tablespoon instant espresso powder (optional)

1½ teaspoons kosher salt

1 cup all-purpose flour

½ cup unsweetened cocoa powder

Cheesecake Layer

2 (16-ounce) packages of cream cheese, at room temperature

½ cup sugar

2 large egg yolks

1 teaspoon pure vanilla extract

½ cup mini chocolate chips, for topping

1. Preheat the oven to 350°F with a rack in the center position. Grease a sheet pan with nonstick spray.

2. MAKE THE BROWNIE LAYER: In a medium saucepan, melt the butter and chocolate chips together over medium-low heat, stirring often, until smooth. Allow to cool for 10 minutes.

3. In a large bowl, whisk the eggs until smooth and foamy, 1 to 2 minutes. Add the sugar and whisk until well combined. Add the chocolate mixture and whisk until smooth. Add the vanilla, espresso powder, if using, and salt, whisking well until shiny and smooth, about 1 minute. Sift in the flour and cocoa powder and fold gently with a rubber spatula until the batter comes together and no streaks remain.

4. Pour the brownie batter into the prepared pan and spread it evenly to the corners with a large offset spatula.

5. MAKE THE CHEESECAKE LAYER: In the bowl of a stand mixer fitted with the paddle attachment or in a large bowl with a handheld mixer, beat the cream cheese and sugar together on medium-high speed until smooth and creamy, about 3 minutes. Add the egg yolks and vanilla and beat until very smooth, 3 minutes more.

6. Use a small ice cream scoop or large spoon to drop dollops of the cream cheese mixture on top of the brownie batter, spacing the drops evenly. Use a knife, toothpick, or offset spatula to swirl the cheesecake layer throughout the brownie layer. Sprinkle the chocolate chips on top. Bake the bars for 18 to 20 minutes, until the cheesecake mixture just starts to brown and a tester inserted into the center comes out with just a few moist crumbs attached. Allow the brownies to cool completely in the pan, about 30 minutes.

7. Slice into pieces, wiping the knife between cuts to help ensure clean lines. The bars will keep, tightly covered, in the refrigerator for up to 4 days.

Key Lime Pie Bars

MAKES 24 BARS

Fresh key lime pie bars are the most joy-inducing treat. I dare you to bite into a cool, creamy square and not be transported to a warmer, friendlier, all-around happier place. Yes, to make a giant pan of key lime pie bars, you'll need to zest and juice a few limes (okay, probably five regular limes, or more if you're using actual key limes), but I promise, the sore wrist is worth it. I won't even ask you to make a curd! Just quickly whisk together a few ingredients, and the fresh lime custard is ready to be poured into the press-in graham cracker and almond crust. The resulting bars are smooth, velvety, and punchy with fresh lime flavor, guaranteed to take you to that happy place.

Crust

Nonstick cooking spray

18 graham crackers

1 cup salted almonds

2 tablespoons granulated sugar

10 tablespoons (1¼ sticks) unsalted butter, melted

Filling

4 (14-ounce) cans sweetened condensed milk

1 cup sour cream

4 tablespoons lime zest (from about 5 regular or 10 key limes)

1½ cups fresh lime juice (from about 6 regular or 12 key limes)

2 large egg yolks

Whipped Cream

1½ cups heavy cream

2 tablespoons confectioners' sugar

1. MAKE THE CRUST: Preheat the oven to 350°F with a rack in the center position. Grease a sheet pan with nonstick spray.

2. Pulse the graham crackers, almonds, and granulated sugar together in a food processor until crumbly and combined, about 1 minute. Add the melted butter and pulse until the mixture resembles wet sand.

3. Press the crumbs firmly and evenly against the bottom of the prepared pan with a flat-bottomed measuring cup. Bake the crust for 10 minutes, until just set and fragrant. Allow to cool for 10 minutes.

4. MEANWHILE, MAKE THE FILLING: In a large bowl, whisk together the condensed milk, sour cream, lime zest, lime juice, and egg yolks until smooth and creamy. Pour the filling into the crust.

5. Carefully transfer the pan back to the oven to bake for 15 minutes, until starting to firm up but still slightly jiggly. Allow the key lime pie to cool at room temperature for 15 minutes, then transfer, uncovered, to the refrigerator and chill for at least 2 hours, or up to overnight.

6. JUST BEFORE SERVING, MAKE THE WHIPPED CREAM: In the bowl of a stand mixer fitted with the whisk attachment or in a large bowl with a handheld mixer, whip the cream and confectioners' sugar on medium-high speed until medium-stiff peaks form, about 5 minutes. Transfer the whipped cream to a piping bag fitted with a star tip.

7. Remove the key lime pie bars from the refrigerator and pipe the whipped cream decoratively on top (alternatively, skip the piping bag and just dollop the whipped cream atop the bars). Slice into pieces. The bars will keep, tightly covered, in the refrigerator for up to 4 days.

Black & White Cookie Bars

MAKES 24 BARS

One of my favorite things about New York City is the ability to find a black and white cookie at pretty much any corner deli or bodega (usually shrink-wrapped and possibly sitting on the shelf just a smidge too long). When I lived in NYC, I used to gravitate toward these dual-frosted beauties like a moth to flame, but now that I live in Seattle, I've had to start making my own. These bars are a fun way to make a lot of black and white cookies at once, without all the fuss of shaping and frosting each one individually. They've got the original's classic cakelike texture, light lemon flavor, and character-istic cap of chocolate and vanilla glazes. You can either glaze half the bars with vanilla and half with chocolate (kind of like making one giant cookie), or stripe the glazes across the pan so that each bar has a good mix of both flavors.

Cookie Base

Nonstick cooking spray

3 cups all-purpose flour

1 teaspoon kosher salt

½ teaspoon baking powder

1 cup (2 sticks) unsalted butter, at room temperature

1¾ cups granulated sugar

4 large eggs

2 tablespoons canola oil

2 teaspoons pure vanilla extract

½ teaspoon pure almond extract

Zest of 1 lemon

1½ cups whole milk

Glaze

½ cup very hot water, plus more as needed

4 cups confectioners' sugar

1 teaspoon fresh lemon juice

1 teaspoon light corn syrup

1 whole vanilla bean, seeds scraped (see tip, page 126)

3 ounces unsweetened chocolate, roughly chopped

1. MAKE THE COOKIE BASE: Preheat the oven to 375°F with a rack in the center position. Grease a sheet pan with nonstick spray.

2. In a medium bowl, whisk together the flour, salt, and baking powder.

3. In the bowl of a stand mixer fitted with the paddle attachment or in a large bowl with a handheld mixer, cream together the butter and granulated sugar on high speed until light and fluffy, about 3 minutes. Add the eggs one at a time, beating on medium speed and scraping down the sides of the bowl after each addition until fully incorporated. Add the oil, vanilla, almond extract, and lemon zest and beat to combine. Add half the flour mixture and mix on low speed until just incorporated. Mix in the milk, then add the rest of the flour and mix just until the batter is smooth. Do not overmix.

4. Pour the batter into the prepared pan and spread it evenly to the corners with a large offset spatula. Bake the cookie base for 15 to 20 minutes, or until a tester inserted into the center comes out clean (the cookie won't take on much color, but will just start to become golden in spots). Allow to cool completely in the pan, about 25 minutes.

5. MEANWHILE, MAKE THE GLAZE: In a large, heatproof bowl, whisk the hot water into the confectioners' sugar, mixing vigor-ously to combine and smooth any lumps. Add the lemon juice, corn syrup, and vanilla bean seeds and whisk to combine. The icing should be thick but easily spreadable; if it's drying out quickly or looks too thick, just add more hot water by the teaspoon until the right consistency is reached.

recipe continues

6. Pour half the glaze over half the cookie base, spreading it evenly to the edges with a large offset spatula. Add the chopped chocolate to the remaining glaze in the bowl and set the bowl over a pot of boiling water to create a double boiler. Stir until all of the chocolate has melted, 3 to 5 minutes (the glaze should thicken, but still be pourable; add more hot water 1 teaspoon at a time if it seems too thick). Pour the chocolate glaze over the other half of the cookie base, spreading it evenly to the edges. Allow the glaze to set for 10 minutes.

7. Slice into pieces. The bars are best the day they are made, but will keep, tightly covered, at room temperature for 3 to 4 days.

How Do I: **Scrape Seeds from a Vanilla Bean?**

To free the precious, flavor-packed seeds from a whole vanilla bean, lay the pod down on a cutting board, hold one end of the bean down, and use a paring knife to split the bean in half lengthwise. Use the dull side of the knife to scrape the cut sides of each half, letting the sticky seeds collect on the end of the knife, then just scrape the seeds straight into the recipe. Don't throw away the pod! Use it to flavor sugar or to make vanilla extract (see page 17).

Pecan Pie Bars

MAKES 24 BARS

A sweet, press-in piecrust and a deep, maple-y pecan filling make these bars a wonderful way to feed pecan pie to the masses. The rich and complex flavors of toasted pecans, maple syrup, brown sugar, and molasses unite to make these bars sing. If you prefer black-bottom pecan pie (if you're my uncle Bob, for example), feel free to replace 1 cup of the nuts with chocolate chips—just scatter them over the crust with the pecans in step 6. Making these bars will leave you with plenty of leftover egg whites, so consider saving them to make a Mint Chocolate Chip Meringue Roll (page 81), Blackberry Coconut Macaroons (page 149), or Eton's Largest Mess (page 186).

6 cups pecans, roughly chopped

Crust

1½ cups (3 sticks) unsalted butter, at room temperature

¾ cup granulated sugar

2 large eggs

2 teaspoons pure vanilla extract

4 cups all-purpose flour

1½ teaspoons kosher salt

3 tablespoons cold water

Filling

1½ cups pure maple syrup

1½ cups packed brown sugar

¾ cup heavy cream

6 tablespoons (¾ stick) unsalted butter

1½ teaspoons kosher salt

2 tablespoons unsulfured molasses (not blackstrap)

9 large egg yolks

1. Preheat the oven to 425°F with a rack in the center position.

2. Spread the pecans in an even layer on a sheet pan and toast in the oven for about 6 minutes, until fragrant. Remove from the oven and allow the pecans to cool for about 15 minutes, then transfer to a large bowl. Reserve the sheet pan.

3. MAKE THE CRUST: In the bowl of a stand mixer fitted with the paddle attachment or in a large bowl with a handheld mixer, cream together the butter and granulated sugar until fluffy and light. Add the eggs and vanilla and beat until smooth. Add the flour and salt and mix on low speed until a crumbly dough forms. Add the cold water 1 tablespoon at a time, mixing on low speed until a smooth dough comes together.

4. Press the dough evenly against the bottom and up the sides of the sheet pan. Chill the crust in the refrigerator while you make the filling.

5. In a heavy-bottomed medium saucepan, combine the maple syrup, brown sugar, cream, butter, and salt. Warm over medium heat, stirring gently, until the butter has melted, about 8 minutes. Remove the pan from the heat and allow to cool for 5 minutes. Whisk in the molasses and egg yolks until smooth.

6. Scatter the toasted pecans evenly over the bottom of the chilled crust and gently pour the filling over the nuts, making sure it reaches all the way to the corners of the pan.

7. Carefully transfer the pan to the oven and immediately reduce the temperature to 325°F. Bake the pie bars for 25 to 30 minutes, until the crust is light golden brown and the center just barely jiggles.

8. Allow the pie bars to cool completely in the pan, about 30 minutes.

9. Slice into pieces. The bars will keep, tightly covered, in the refrigerator for up to a week.

Six-Layer Dolly Bars

MAKES 24 BARS

Sometimes called magic bars or Hello, Dolly bars, these supremely sweet and simple squares are made with just a handful of ingredients, usually chocolate, coconut, and nuts, held together by some butter and a can of sweetened condensed milk. The ingredients melt together beautifully in the oven, transforming into a truly decadent treat—rich, chocolaty, crunchy, and gooey all at once, perfect for a little after-school pick-me-up. I love the combination of salty pretzels, crunchy coconut, nutty cashews, and sweet dried pineapple, but this recipe is easily adaptable, so feel free to swap in your favorite flavors.

Nonstick cooking spray

6 heaping cups thin pretzel twists

1 cup (2 sticks) unsalted butter, melted

2 (14-ounce) cans sweetened condensed milk

2 cups unsweetened coconut flakes, toasted (see headnote, page 33)

3 cups bittersweet chocolate chips

1 cup finely chopped dried pineapple

1 cup roasted, unsalted whole cashews, roughly chopped

1. Preheat the oven to 350°F with a rack in the center position. Grease a sheet pan with nonstick spray.

2. In a food processor, pulse the pretzels into coarse crumbs. Add the melted butter and pulse until the mixture resembles wet sand.

3. Pour the pretzel crumbs onto the prepared pan and use your palms or a flat-bottomed measuring cup to press in an even layer to cover the bottom of the pan all the way to the corners (it will seem thin). Pour the condensed milk evenly over the pretzel layer, then scatter the coconut, chocolate chips, dried pineapple, and cashews on top. Press gently with a fork to adhere. Bake for 15 to 18 minutes, until the bars are starting to brown and just bubbling. Allow the bars to cool completely in the pan, about 30 minutes.

4. Use a sharp knife to slice into pieces. The bars will keep, tightly covered, in the refrigerator for up to a week.

Cookies

For the Jar

Cookies? On a sheet pan? Groundbreaking. But honestly, name a better duo! Some things we just know to be true: Bert goes with Ernie, Michelle goes with Barack, and cookies belong on a sheet pan. Facts!

When it comes to portability, snackability, or just general joy and nostalgia, you can't really beat the cookie. Whether it's thick or thin, chewy or cakey, filled with nuts or melty chocolate chips, coated in sparkly sugar, or sandwiched together with a bit of buttercream, there's a 98 percent chance that you're going to enjoy it. Scientifically. Maybe.

There are a million wonderful cookies out there in the world, so when choosing the cookie recipes to include here, I wanted a variety of flavors, textures, and techniques and, of course, I wanted ease and approachability. I included my personal go-tos, culled my family archives, and honed some new-to-me ideas, and I think I've hit all the marks. There are great options for sweet after-school snacks (check out the Kitchen Sink Cookies, page 134), holiday cookie swaps (Molasses Sparkle Cookies, page 161), midmorning pick-me-ups (Matcha Crinkles, page 142), or just a little rainy afternoon coziness (I'm in for a Tahini Brownie Cookie, page 139). I hope you enjoy them all just as much as I do!

A few tips for cookie baking success: First, use an ice cream scoop to portion the cookie dough—it's cleaner than using two spoons or fingers and ensures that each cookie is exactly the same size and shape. My second tip is, if you don't want to make a whole batch of cookies at once, try scooping the dough into balls and flash-freezing the unbaked dough on a pan. Transfer the frozen dough balls to a labeled bag and stash them in the freezer, where you can revel in the possibility of baking off as many as you like whenever a fresh, hot cookie strikes your fancy. (If you take this advice and bake a batch from frozen, just be sure to add a minute or two to the bake time.)

Okay, have we covered all our cookie bases? Let's get baking.

Kitchen Sink Cookies

MAKES 40 TO
45 COOKIES

The development of these cookies was a happy accident, when I'd run out of all-purpose flour but wanted to use up all the half-empty bags of bits and bobs in my cupboard. Behold, my kitchen sinkers, chock-full of sweet and salty goodies and naturally gluten-free. These are quite adaptable, so if you prefer butterscotch chips over peanut butter or pretzel bits over peanuts, feel free to adjust the recipe accordingly. And if you can't find oat or almond flour, it's easy to make your own by blitzing rolled oats or whole almonds in a food processor until very finely ground (just don't overprocess the almonds into nut butter).

2 cups almond flour

2½ cups oat flour

1 teaspoon baking soda

1 teaspoon baking powder

1 teaspoon kosher salt

1 cup (2 sticks) unsalted butter, at room temperature

1 cup granulated sugar

1 cup packed dark brown sugar

2 large eggs

1 large egg yolk

1 tablespoon pure vanilla extract

1 cup candy-coated chocolates (I like M&M's), plus more for topping

1 cup peanut butter chips, plus more for topping

½ cup toffee bits, plus more for topping

½ cup dry-roasted peanuts, plus more for topping

Flaky sea salt, such as Maldon

Nonstick baking spray

1. Preheat the oven to 350°F with a rack in the center position. Line two sheet pans, or as many as you have, with parchment paper.

2. In a medium bowl, whisk together the almond and oat flours, baking soda, baking powder, and kosher salt.

3. In the bowl of a stand mixer fitted with the paddle attachment or in a large bowl with a handheld mixer, cream together the butter, granulated sugar, and brown sugar on medium-high speed until fluffy and combined, about 3 minutes. Add the eggs and egg yolk one at a time, beating until smooth and scraping down the sides of the bowl after each addition, about 3 minutes. Add the vanilla and beat until incorporated. Add the dry ingredients and mix on low speed until the dough comes together. Add the candy-coated chocolates, peanut butter chips, toffee bits, and peanuts and mix on low speed until well incorporated.

4. Sprinkle about 8 small mounds of flaky sea salt on each of the prepared pans, spacing them about 2 inches apart (this is where the cookie dough will go). Use a 2-tablespoon scoop to portion the dough into balls and place the balls on top of the flaky salt mounds. Grease your hand with nonstick baking spray and gently press down on each dough ball to flatten slightly. Top with a few extra candy-coated chocolates, toffee bits, peanut butter chips, or peanuts.

5. Bake the cookies for about 8 minutes, until just golden around the edges. Set the sheet pans on a wire rack and let the cookies cool completely on the pans, about 10 minutes. Repeat with any remaining dough.

6. Store the cookies in an airtight container at room temperature for up to 5 days.

Cardamom Snickerdoodles

MAKES ABOUT
30 COOKIES

Snickerdoodle. *The name alone is reason to smile—and just wait until you bite into one. Soft, sweet, and lightly spiced, snickerdoodles have a way of making you feel like a kid again, especially when served with a glass of cold milk. I've added cardamom to these for an inviting twist, but if it's nostalgia you're after, you can replace the cardamom with ground cinnamon for a more traditional flavor profile.*

2¾ cups all-purpose flour

2 teaspoons baking powder

½ teaspoon kosher salt

1 cup (2 sticks) unsalted butter, at room temperature

1¾ cups sugar

2 large eggs

1 teaspoon pure vanilla extract

2 tablespoons ground cardamom

1. Preheat the oven to 350°F with a rack in the center position. Line two sheet pans, or as many as you have, with parchment paper.

2. In a medium bowl, whisk together the flour, baking powder, and salt.

3. In the bowl of a stand mixer fitted with the paddle attachment or in a large bowl with a handheld mixer, cream together the butter and 1½ cups of the sugar on medium-high speed until fluffy and combined, about 3 minutes. Add the eggs one at a time, beating until incorporated and scraping down the sides of bowl after each addition. Beat in the vanilla. Add the dry ingredients and beat on low speed just until the dough comes together without any streaks.

4. In a small bowl, whisk together the remaining ¼ cup sugar and the cardamom.

5. Use a 1½-tablespoon scoop to portion the dough into balls, then roll in the cardamom sugar until well coated. Arrange the dough balls on the prepared pans, spacing them about 2 inches apart, 6 to 8 cookies per pan. Use your hand or the bottom of a glass to gently press down on the tops of the dough balls to flatten. Bake the cookies for about 8 minutes, until the sides are just beginning to brown. Allow the cookies to cool on the pans for 5 minutes, then transfer to a wire rack to cool completely, about 5 minutes more. Repeat with any remaining dough.

6. Store the cookies in an airtight container at room temperature for up to 4 days.

Flourless Peanut Butter Oaties

MAKES 18 TO 20
COOKIES

At the start of the pandemic, when a bag of flour seemed nearly impossible to find, my kids and I made versions of these soft, chewy, flourless peanut butter cookies on repeat. We started with Shauna Sever's Giant Awesome Peanut Butter Cookie recipe from her beautiful book Midwest Made*, adding to and tweaking it over and over again depending on what we had in the pantry. This version, stuffed with oats and rolled in crunchy turbinado sugar, is one of my favorite iterations. Be sure to use processed peanut butter here to ensure a soft, gorgeous texture.*

2 cups creamy peanut butter

1 cup packed brown sugar

½ teaspoon kosher salt

4 tablespoons (½ stick) unsalted butter, melted and cooled

2 large eggs

1 teaspoon pure vanilla extract

1 teaspoon baking soda

1 cup rolled oats

Turbinado sugar

Flaky sea salt, such as Maldon

1. Preheat the oven to 350°F with a rack in the center position. Line two sheet pans, or as many as you have, with parchment paper.

2. In the bowl of a stand mixer fitted with the paddle attachment or in a large bowl with a handheld mixer, beat together the peanut butter, brown sugar, kosher salt, and melted butter on high speed until smooth, about 2 minutes. Add the eggs one at a time, beating on medium-low speed and scraping down the sides of the bowl after each addition until fully incorporated, then beat in the vanilla. Stir in the baking soda and oats on low speed until the dough is homogeneous.

3. Use a 2-tablespoon scoop to portion the dough into balls, then roll each ball in turbinado sugar to coat completely. Place the dough balls on the prepared pans, spacing them about 2 inches apart, about 8 per pan. Use a fork to flatten the dough balls and give the cookies their cross-hatched pattern. Sprinkle each cookie with a pinch of flaky sea salt. Bake for 8 to 9 minutes, until the cookies are golden and the edges look just set (they will seem underdone, but will continue to set up as they cool). Set the sheet pans on a wire rack and let the cookies cool completely on the pans, about 10 minutes. Repeat with any remaining dough.

4. Store the cookies in an airtight container at room temperature for up to 3 days.

Tahini Brownie Cookies

MAKES 25 TO
30 COOKIES

These are rich, fudgy brownies in cookie form, which means that every piece is an edge piece, ya feel? Tahini, a smooth sesame paste popular in Middle Eastern and Mediterranean cooking, helps make a lovely, sweet, and nutty glaze to offset the deeply chocolaty cookies. Note that this batter needs time to firm up before baking, so mix up the dough at least 30 minutes (or up to a day or two) before you want to serve the cookies.

Brownie Cookies

½ cup (1 stick) unsalted butter

6 ounces bittersweet chocolate chips (about 1 cup)

1 cup granulated sugar

¼ cup packed brown sugar

3 large eggs

1 teaspoon pure vanilla extract

½ teaspoon baking soda

½ teaspoon kosher salt

¼ cup plus 2 tablespoons unsweetened cocoa powder

¾ cup all-purpose flour

Tahini Glaze

¼ cup tahini, stirred well

2 tablespoons whole milk

½ cup confectioners' sugar

Sesame seeds (optional)

1. MAKE THE BROWNIE COOKIES: In a medium pot, melt the butter over medium heat. Turn off the heat and add the chocolate chips, stirring gently with a rubber spatula until melted and smooth. Whisk in the granulated sugar and brown sugar until smooth. Add the eggs and vanilla and whisk until smooth and glossy. Stir in the baking soda and salt. Sift in the cocoa powder and flour and stir gently with the rubber spatula until incorporated and the dough is thick and smooth (it will look like brownie batter).

2. Cover the pot with plastic wrap and chill the dough in the refrigerator overnight (alternatively, if you don't want to wait that long, you can transfer it to a large bowl and refrigerate, uncovered, for 30 to 60 minutes).

3. Preheat the oven to 350°F with a rack in the center position. Line two sheet pans, or as many as you have, with parchment paper.

4. Use a 1½-tablespoon scoop to portion the dough into balls and arrange on the prepared pans, spacing them about 2 inches apart, about 8 per pan. Bake the cookies for about 9 minutes, until just set around the edges (they will spread and seem just underdone in the centers, but will continue to firm up as they cool). Set the sheet pans on a wire rack and let the cookies cool completely on the pans, about 12 minutes. Repeat with any remaining dough.

5. MAKE THE TAHINI GLAZE: In a medium bowl, whisk together the tahini, milk, and confectioners' sugar until smooth.

6. Generously drizzle the tahini glaze over the cooled cookies and sprinkle lightly with sesame seeds, if using. Allow the glaze to firm up, about 10 to 15 minutes, before serving.

7. Store the cookies in an airtight container between layers of parchment paper at room temperature for up to 3 days.

photograph follows

Matcha Crinkles

Matcha, a strong and handsomely verdant Japanese green tea powder, has been having a real moment lately, flavoring everything from lattes and smoothies to cakes and ice cream. Celebrated for its highly antioxidant properties, matcha has a slightly bitter, grassy flavor, which pairs beautifully with sweet white chocolate and brown sugar in these gorgeously green cookies. They're a welcome midmorning or early afternoon pick-me-up on those days when you just need a little jolt of sweetness (and maybe a bit of caffeine, too).

Note: You'll find two types of matcha powder available for purchase: ceremonial and culinary-grade (ceremonial matcha is sweeter, mellower, and pricier than culinary-grade matcha). Either will work for this recipe; just be sure it's unsweetened.

1⅔ cups all-purpose flour

1 teaspoon baking powder

¼ teaspoon baking soda

¾ cup plus 3 tablespoons granulated sugar

½ cup packed brown sugar

2 large eggs

2 large egg yolks

1 teaspoon pure vanilla extract

½ teaspoon kosher salt

5 tablespoons unsalted butter

4 ounces white chocolate chips

3 tablespoons unsweetened matcha powder

½ cup confectioners' sugar

1. In a medium bowl, whisk together the flour, baking powder, and baking soda.

2. In a large bowl, whisk together ¾ cup of the granulated sugar, the brown sugar, eggs, egg yolks, vanilla, and salt until well combined and slightly frothy.

3. In a small saucepan over medium-low heat, melt the butter and white chocolate together, stirring often with a rubber spatula, until smooth. Whisk in the matcha powder until thoroughly combined.

4. Whisk the matcha mixture into the egg and sugar mixture until smooth and homogeneous. Fold in the dry ingredients until the cookie dough comes together and no streaks remain. Let the dough rest at room temperature or in the refrigerator for at least 10 minutes, or up to 2 hours, to hydrate and firm up a bit.

5. Preheat the oven to 350°F with a rack in the center position. Line two sheet pans, or as many as you have, with parchment paper.

6. In a small bowl, whisk together the confectioners' sugar and remaining 3 tablespoons granulated sugar.

7. Use a 1½-tablespoon scoop to portion the dough into balls and roll in the sugar mixture until well coated. Arrange the dough balls on the prepared pans, spacing them about 2 inches apart, 6 or 7 per pan. Bake the cookies for 8 minutes, until the tops are crackly and the sides are just beginning to brown.

8. Allow the cookies to cool on the pans for about 5 minutes, then transfer to a wire rack to cool completely, about 5 minutes more. Repeat with any remaining dough.

9. The cookies are best the day they are made, but will keep, in an airtight container between layers of parchment paper, at room temperature up to 3 days.

White Chocolate Gingerbread Cookies

MAKES 30 TO 35 COOKIES

Warm and cozy gingerbread spices meet sweet white chocolate in these easy (and slightly addicting) cookies. Whether tucked into a lunch box, gifted to neighbors, or left out on a plate for Santa, these beauties are guaranteed to land you on the nice list.

3 cups all-purpose flour

1 teaspoon baking soda

1 teaspoon kosher salt

1 teaspoon ground cinnamon

1 teaspoon ground ginger

¼ teaspoon ground cloves

1 cup (2 sticks) unsalted butter, at room temperature

1 cup packed dark brown sugar

½ cup granulated sugar

2 large eggs

2 teaspoons pure vanilla extract

¼ cup unsulfured molasses (not blackstrap)

12 ounces (about 2 cups) chopped white chocolate or white chocolate chips

Flaky sea salt, such as Maldon

1. Preheat the oven to 350°F with a rack in the center position. Line two sheet pans, or as many as you have, with parchment paper.

2. In a medium bowl, whisk together the flour, baking soda, kosher salt, cinnamon, ginger, and cloves.

3. In the bowl of a stand mixer fitted with the paddle attachment or in a large bowl with a handheld mixer, cream together the butter, brown sugar, and granulated sugar on medium-high speed until fluffy and well combined, about 3 minutes. Add the eggs one at a time, beating until smooth and scraping down the sides of the bowl after each addition. Add the vanilla and molasses and mix on medium speed until incorporated, about 1 minute. Add the dry ingredients and mix on low speed just until the dough comes together, 1 minute more. Fold in the white chocolate chips with a rubber spatula.

4. Use a 2-tablespoon scoop to portion the dough into balls. Place the balls on the prepared pans, spacing them about 2 inches apart, about 8 per pan. Sprinkle each dough ball with a pinch of flaky sea salt. Bake for 8 to 11 minutes, until the cookies are starting to brown around the edges and just barely set in the centers. Set the sheet pans on a wire rack and let the cookies cool completely on the pans, about 12 minutes. Repeat with any remaining dough.

5. Store the cookies in an airtight container at room temperature for 3 to 4 days.

Chocolate Chip Cookie Brittle

SERVES 8 TO 10

If you prefer crisp and buttery chocolate chip cookies over the thick and cakey variety, this brittle is for you. Using chopped chocolate instead of chips gives the perfect distribution of chocolate flavor, and a good sprinkle of flaky salt rounds out the sweet, caramel-y cookie flavor. What results are crisp, buttery shards of chocolate chip cookie perfection. Fair warning: It's entirely too easy to wolf down the whole pan in one go.

Nonstick baking spray

1¼ cups (2½ sticks) unsalted butter, at room temperature

½ cup granulated sugar

½ cup packed brown sugar

1 tablespoon pure vanilla extract

1 teaspoon kosher salt

2 cups all-purpose flour

1½ cups chopped dark chocolate

1 tablespoon flaky sea salt, such as Maldon

1. Preheat the oven to 375°F with a rack in the center position. Grease a sheet pan with nonstick spray.

2. In the bowl of a stand mixer fitted with the paddle attachment or in a large bowl with a handheld mixer, cream together the butter, granulated sugar, and brown sugar until light and fluffy, about 3 minutes. Add the vanilla and salt and beat to combine. With the mixer on low speed, stir in the flour, then the chopped chocolate, until the dough just comes together.

3. Transfer the dough to the prepared pan. Use lightly greased hands to press the dough evenly into the pan, all the way to the corners. Sprinkle the flaky sea salt generously over the top. Bake the brittle for 18 to 20 minutes, until deeply golden. Allow the brittle to cool completely in the pan, about 30 minutes.

4. Break the brittle into uneven shards. Store in an airtight container at room temperature for up to 5 days.

Blackberry Coconut Macaroons

MAKES ABOUT
25 COOKIES

Usually, I'm inclined to skip the macaroons on the Passover table, as the ones from a box (or a cylindrical tube—you know the ones) tend to be one-note bombs of cloying sweetness. Homemade macaroons are a different story, though, and these particular macaroons, the idea for which came from (who else?) Deb Perelman of Smitten Kitchen, *are an entirely different story. These little coconut bundles are light textured, almost creamy, with clear coconut flavor and some much-needed tartness from fresh berries. Deb uses raspberries, but I love the deep purple that fresh blackberries bring, and I find that a hint of lemon zest helps tie all the flavors together nicely. They're extra wonderful with a drizzle of dark chocolate on top, if the mood strikes, though they certainly don't need it, and they need not be limited to the Passover table—they're delicious anytime of year.*

1 (14-ounce) bag sweetened shredded coconut

⅔ cup sugar

3 large egg whites

½ teaspoon kosher salt

½ teaspoon pure almond extract

½ teaspoon pure vanilla extract

Zest of 1 lemon

½ pint fresh blackberries

1. Preheat the oven to 325°F with a rack in the center position. Line a sheet pan with parchment paper.

2. Add the coconut to a food processor. Pulse for about 1 minute, until the coconut breaks down to a chunky paste. Add the sugar, egg whites, salt, almond extract, vanilla, and lemon zest and pulse until very well incorporated, about 1 minute. Add the blackberries and pulse 10 times, until the berries have started to break down and incorporate into the coconut but are still chunky in spots.

3. Use a 1½-tablespoon scoop to portion the dough into balls, making sure to get a bit of purple dough and a bit of white dough in each scoop. Arrange the dough balls onto the prepared pan, leaving a scant inch of space between each. Bake the macaroons for about 30 minutes, until dry and lightly browned. Set the sheet pan on a wire rack and let the macaroons cool completely on the pan, about 25 minutes.

4. Store the macaroons in an airtight container at room temperature for up 3 days, or in the freezer for up to 3 months.

Chocolate Meringue Kisses

MAKES ABOUT
30 COOKIES

Don't let these sweet and dainty meringue cookies fool you—they pack some serious chocolate flavor in that cute little kiss-shaped bundle. The meringue whips up fairly quickly, but the cookies bake low and slow in the oven, which allows the outsides to dry out and become crisp while the insides remain slightly soft and marshmallow-y. A dunk in a pool of melted chocolate or even just a drizzle finishes them off, and I can't be held responsible for how many you might eat in one sitting.

3 large egg whites

Cream of tartar

Kosher salt

¾ cup sugar

2 teaspoons unsweetened cocoa powder

1 teaspoon pure vanilla extract

4 ounces bittersweet chocolate, chopped, or chocolate chips

1 teaspoon coconut oil

1. Preheat the oven to 200°F with a rack in the center position. Line a sheet pan or two with parchment paper.

2. In the bowl of a stand mixer fitted with the whisk attachment or in a large bowl with a handheld mixer, whip together the egg whites, a pinch of cream of tartar, and a pinch of salt on medium-high speed until opaque, soft peaks form, 2 to 3 minutes. Slowly add the sugar and whip until the meringue is stiff and glossy, about 3 minutes more. Sift the cocoa powder into the bowl and add the vanilla, then fold with a rubber spatula until combined. Scoop the meringue into a large piping bag fitted with a ½-inch star tip.

3. Pipe 1-inch-wide meringue stars onto the prepared pan(s), leaving just ½ inch of space between the stars (alternatively, if you don't have a piping bag, scoop 1-inch mounds of meringue on the sheet pan with a cookie scoop or large spoon). Bake the meringue kisses for 1½ to 2 hours, until firm and dry. Turn off the oven and prop open the door with a wooden spoon handle, then let the meringues cool completely inside, about 2 hours, or up to overnight.

4. Once the meringues have cooled, melt the chocolate and coconut oil together in a small pot over low heat, about 8 minutes. (Alternatively, melt in a medium microwave-safe bowl in 30-second intervals in the microwave, stirring between, 1 to 2 minutes total.) Stir the chocolate and oil together until no lumps remain.

5. Dip the flat side of each meringue in the melted chocolate, then return to the sheet pan(s), or drizzle the melted chocolate artfully over the meringues, or write a secret message. Allow the chocolate to set at room temperature, about 1 hour, or in the refrigerator, about 10 minutes.

6. Store the meringue kisses in an airtight container at room temperature for up to 4 days.

Chocolate Hazelnut Palmiers

MAKES ABOUT
20 COOKIES

These sugar-dusted heart-shaped cookies, sometimes called palm hearts or elephant ears, are so easy to make using store-bought frozen puff pastry. They're usually assembled just with sugar, or sometimes with a thin layer of jam, but adding a drizzle of chocolate hazelnut spread just feels like the right thing to do, somehow. As they bake, the sugar and chocolate start to caramelize, giving these little laminated cookies a deep, nutty flavor and wonderfully crisp texture. Bonus points for the short and pantry-friendly ingredient list!

1 cup sugar

¼ teaspoon kosher salt

1 sheet frozen puff pastry, thawed

¼ cup chocolate hazelnut spread, such as Nutella

1. Preheat the oven to 450°F with a rack in the center position. Line two sheet pans with parchment paper.

2. In a small bowl, whisk together the sugar and salt. Scatter ½ cup of the sugar mixture over a work surface and place the sheet of puff pastry on top. Sprinkle the remaining ½ cup sugar mixture over the puff pastry. Use a rolling pin to roll the puff pastry out to a 13-inch square, pressing the sugar into the dough.

3. In a small microwave-safe bowl, warm the Nutella in the microwave for 30 to 45 seconds, until pourable. Drizzle the Nutella evenly over the puff pastry.

4. Fold the left and right sides of the puff pastry square in toward the center, stopping halfway to the middle of the pastry. Then fold in the sides again so the two folds meet at the center line. Finally, fold one side over the other, as if closing a book, so you have a long log of folded dough. Use a sharp knife to slice the dough log crosswise into ¾-inch-thick slices.

5. Place the palmiers cut side up on the prepared pans, spacing them about 2 inches apart; you should be able to fit about 10 per pan. Bake the palmiers for 8 minutes, flipping halfway through, until well browned and caramelized around the edges. Let the palmiers cool completely on the pans, about 12 minutes.

6. Store the palmiers in an airtight container at room temperature for up to 4 days.

Café Latte Cookies

MAKES ABOUT
20 COOKIES

How do you take your coffee? Black? Extra milky? How about in cookie form? Like a grown-up chocolate chip cookie, these buzzy little numbers are made with instant espresso powder and white chocolate and are the perfect solution for those mid-afternoon, could-use-some-coffee-but-also-make-it-sweet cravings.

1⅔ cups all-purpose flour

1 teaspoon baking powder

¼ teaspoon baking soda

½ teaspoon kosher salt

¾ cup granulated sugar

½ cup packed brown sugar

2 large eggs

2 large egg yolks

1 teaspoon pure vanilla extract

5 tablespoons unsalted butter

3 ounces white chocolate

¼ cup instant espresso powder

1 cup white chocolate chips or chopped white chocolate

Confectioners' sugar

1. In a medium bowl, whisk together the flour, baking powder, baking soda, and salt.

2. In a large bowl, vigorously whisk together the granulated sugar, brown sugar, eggs, egg yolks, and vanilla until smooth.

3. In a small saucepan over low heat, melt together the butter and white chocolate, stirring frequently until smooth, about 8 minutes (alternatively, melt in a medium microwave-safe bowl in the microwave in 30-second intervals, stirring between, about 2 minutes total). Remove the pot from the heat and whisk in the espresso powder until completely combined.

4. Add the white chocolate mixture to the egg mixture and whisk until well combined. Fold in the flour mixture until the cookie dough comes together, then fold in the white chocolate chips. Let the dough sit in the refrigerator for about an hour.

5. Preheat the oven to 350°F with a rack in the center position. Line two sheet pans, or as many as you have, with parchment paper.

6. Use a 1½-tablespoon scoop to portion the dough into balls and roll in the confectioners' sugar until fully coated. Place the dough balls on the prepared pans, spacing them about 2 inches apart, about 10 per pan. Bake the cookies for 8 to 10 minutes, until the edges are set but the centers are still a bit soft. Allow the cookies to cool on the pans for 5 minutes, then transfer to a wire rack to cool completely.

7. Store the cookies in an airtight container at room temperature for up to 4 days.

Oatmeal Creme Pies

MAKES 14 SANDWICH
COOKIES

Back in 1996, a Little Debbie Oatmeal Creme Pie was like a walletful of Bitcoin in the middle school lunchroom. Tradeable for anything! While testing this home-made version, I let Stella Parks of BraveTart be my guide—she's done such a fantastic job of converting classic store-bought American treats (Oreos, Girl Scout Cookies, Nutter Butters, etc.) for the home kitchen. I streamlined and adapted Stella's recipe, subbing store-bought marshmallow creme for home-made and golden raisins for dried apples, which are easier for me to find locally. The resulting oatmeal creme pies are sweet and lightly spiced, held together beautifully with a buttery marshmallow fill-ing. Truly lunchroom-worthy.

Oatmeal Cookies

2 cups all-purpose flour

1 cup rolled oats

2 tablespoons unsweetened cocoa powder

⅔ cup golden raisins

½ teaspoon kosher salt

1½ teaspoons baking soda

½ teaspoon baking powder

¼ teaspoon ground nutmeg

¼ teaspoon ground ginger

¼ teaspoon ground cinnamon

10 tablespoons (1¼ sticks) unsalted butter, at room temperature

1 cup packed dark brown sugar

2 tablespoons unsulfored molasses (not blackstrap)

1 large egg

¼ cup whole milk

Marshmallow Creme Filling

½ cup (1 stick) unsalted butter, at room temperature

1 (7-ounce) jar marshmallow creme

Kosher salt

1. MAKE THE OATMEAL COOKIES: Preheat the oven to 350°F with a rack in the center position. Line two sheet pans, or as many as you have, with parchment paper.

2. In a food processor, grind together the flour, oats, cocoa powder, raisins, salt, baking soda, baking powder, nutmeg, ginger, and cin-namon until well combined but still a bit chunky, about 1 minute.

3. In the bowl of a stand mixer fitted with the paddle attachment or in a large bowl with a handheld mixer, cream together the butter and brown sugar on medium-high speed until fluffy, about 3 minutes. Add the molasses and egg and beat until smooth. Reduce the speed to low and add the flour mixture, then the milk, and mix to combine, about 1 minute.

4. Use a 1-tablespoon scoop to portion the cookie dough into balls. Place on the prepared pans, spacing them about 2 inches apart, about 10 per pan. Bake the cookies for 9 to 11 minutes, until puffed and dry around the edges. Allow the cookies to cool completely on the pans, about 10 minutes. Repeat with any remaining dough.

5. MEANWHILE, MAKE THE CREME FILLING: In the bowl of a stand mixer fitted with the paddle attachment or in a large bowl with a handheld mixer, beat together the butter, marshmallow creme, and a pinch of salt on medium-high speed until smooth and creamy, about 3 minutes.

6. Scoop 2 teaspoons of the creme filling onto the undersides of half the oatmeal cookies and top with the remaining cookies to make sandwiches (if you end up with an odd number of cookies, enjoy a chef's treat!).

7. Store the cookies in an airtight container in the refrigerator for 4 to 5 days.

Nana's Kiflings

MAKES ABOUT
20 COOKIES

My mother-in-law, Octavia, who grew up in Lookout Mountain, Tennessee, makes boxes and boxes of kiflings every Christmas, just like her mom (Great-Nana) did before her. In fact, these lovely little treats are a Lookout Mountain cookie tradition generations in the making. Sometimes called almond crescents or kipferl, these nutty, melt-in-your-mouth cookies are similar in taste and texture to Russian tea cakes, Mexican wedding cookies, and snowball cookies. They're simple to make and highly giftable, and their deep, nutty flavor and short, buttery texture, all rolled up in a thick powdered sugar shell, make them impossible to resist. Go on, try one—Nana would insist.

½ cup raw almonds

½ teaspoon kosher salt

¼ cup granulated sugar

14 tablespoons (1¾ sticks) unsalted butter, at room temperature

1 teaspoon pure vanilla extract

1½ cups plus 6 tablespoons all-purpose flour

1 to 2 cups confectioners' sugar

1. Preheat the oven to 300°F with a rack in the center position. Line two sheet pans with parchment paper.

2. Place the almonds and salt in a food processor. Pulse until the almonds are coarsely ground, about 1 minute. Add the granulated sugar, butter, and vanilla and pulse until a thick paste comes together, 1 to 2 minutes. Add the flour and pulse again until just incorporated, about 6 pulses. The dough will seem a bit crumbly, but should clump together when pressed.

3. Use a scoop to portion the dough into scant 1-tablespoon balls, then shape each piece into a crescent moon shape. Place the dough crescents on the prepared pans, spacing them ½ inch apart, about 10 per pan. Bake the kiflings for 35 to 45 minutes, until dry, slightly puffed, and very lightly brown around the edges. Allow the cookies to cool on the pans for 5 to 10 minutes, then roll in the confectioners' sugar to coat generously. Let the sugared cookies cool completely on a wire rack, about 10 minutes more.

4. Store the kiflings in an airtight container at room temperature for up to a week.

Molasses Sparkle Cookies

MAKES ABOUT
20 COOKIES

These sweet and spicy lovelies have been the cornerstone of my holiday cookie tins for at least eight years running—at this point, if I didn't aggressively disperse them throughout the neighborhood come December, I'd probably get concerned knocks on the door from friends and neighbors, asking if everything was okay over here. Have I fallen down? Am I trapped under something heavy? Where are the cookies?! As cookies go, I (and everyone else, it seems) love their warm spice, crunchy raw-sugar-dipped coats, and tender yet sturdy chew. They hold up well for a few days in a cookie tin, and the smell in your kitchen while they're baking? Just pure unadulterated holiday cheer.

2¼ cups all-purpose flour

2 teaspoons baking soda

1 teaspoon ground cinnamon

½ teaspoon ground ginger

½ teaspoon ground allspice

¼ teaspoon ground nutmeg

1 teaspoon kosher salt

¾ cup (1½ sticks) unsalted butter, at room temperature

¾ cup packed light brown sugar

1 large egg

½ cup unsulfured molasses (not blackstrap)

Turbinado sugar

1. In a medium bowl, whisk together the flour, baking soda, cinnamon, ginger, allspice, nutmeg, and salt until combined.

2. In the bowl of a stand mixer fitted with the paddle attachment or in a large bowl with a handheld mixer, cream together the butter and brown sugar until light and fluffy, about 3 minutes. Add the egg and mix to combine. Beat in the molasses, mixing thoroughly for 1 minute. Add the dry ingredients all at once and mix on low speed until the dough comes together. Refrigerate the dough, covered, for at least 1 hour or up to 2 days.

3. Preheat the oven to 375°F with a rack in the center position. Line two sheet pans, or as many as you have, with parchment paper.

4. Use a 1½-tablespoon scoop to portion the dough into balls, then roll each ball in turbinado sugar to coat. Place on the prepared baking sheets, spacing them about 1½ inches apart, about 8 per pan. Slightly flatten each cookie with the palm of your hand. Bake the cookies for 8 to 10 minutes, until deeply golden around the edge. They will look sort of puffy, but will deflate and flatten as they cool. Allow the cookies to cool on the pans for 5 minutes, then transfer to a wire rack to cool completely, about 7 minutes more. Repeat with any remaining dough.

5. Store the cookies in an airtight container at room temperature for up to 5 days.

Tell Me: **What Exactly Is Turbinado Sugar?**

Though it might sound fancy, turbinado sugar is just raw, unrefined sugar. Unlike regular, refined white sugar, granules of turbinado sugar are large, coarse, and light brown in color. These granules don't easily melt into batters while baking, so I find turbinado sugar perfect for creating a sparkly, crunchy, bakery-worthy topping, whether sprinkled over a batch of festive molasses spice cookies, homemade scones, on a fresh pie crust, or atop a simple, snacky cake (like banana bread or my Blueberry Muffin Cake, page 209). At the store, look for *sugar in the raw*, and if you can't find turbinado sugar anywhere, demerara sugar (which is very similar structurally, but has a lighter, less molasses-y flavor) makes a good substitute.

Pecan Caramel Shortbread Cookies

MAKES ABOUT
25 COOKIES

These nutty shortbread thumb-prints are melt-in-your-mouth delicious, held together with a dollop of store-bought dulce de leche, a Latin American caramelized milk jam. If you can't find dulce de leche at the store, it's simple to make your own with a can of sweetened condensed milk, or use a good-quality thick caramel sauce instead. I like to toast the pecans on (you guessed it) a sheet pan—just pop them into the oven at 350°F until brown and fragrant, about 10 minutes.

2 cups pecan halves, toasted (see headnote)

2 cups all-purpose flour

1 cup (2 sticks) unsalted butter, at room temperature

⅓ cup confectioners' sugar

⅓ cup packed dark brown sugar

1 large egg yolk

1 teaspoon kosher salt

2 teaspoons pure vanilla extract

½ teaspoon ground nutmeg

1 (13-ounce) jar dulce de leche

1. Preheat the oven to 350°F with a rack in the center position. Line two sheet pans, or as many as you have, with parchment paper.

2. In a food processor, combine 1½ cups of the pecans with ½ cup of the flour and pulse 10 to 15 times, until well combined and the nuts are no bigger than the size of lentils.

3. In the bowl of a stand mixer fitted with the paddle attachment or in a large bowl with a handheld mixer, cream together the butter, confectioners' sugar, and brown sugar on medium-high speed until fluffy and light, about 3 minutes. Add the egg yolk, salt, and vanilla and beat until smooth, about 1 minute. Add the remaining 1½ cups flour, the nutmeg, and the pecan and flour mixture and mix on low speed just until the dough comes together.

4. Use a 1½-tablespoon scoop to portion the dough into balls. Place on the prepared pans, spacing them 2 inches apart, 8 to 10 per pan. Use a large wooden spoon handle to gently create an indentation on top of each cookie, about ½ inch deep. Bake the cookies for 5 minutes (they'll still look a bit wet), then remove from the oven, press into the indentations with the spoon handle again to better define the divots, then fill each indentation with ½ teaspoon dulce de leche. Place one of the remaining pecan halves on top of each cookie, right over the dulce de leche. Return the pans to the oven and bake for another 5 minutes, until the cookies are set around the edges and the dulce de leche is just starting to bubble. Set the sheet pans on a wire rack and let the cookies cool completely on the pans, about 15 minutes. Repeat with any remaining dough.

5. Store the cookies in an airtight container at room temperature for up to 4 days.

Pies &
the Like

Fruit Forward

Fruity desserts are some of my favorites—a fresh fruit tart, bright and glistening in the window of a patisserie, the crisp crust and juicy sweetness of a simple galette, or a warm scoop of tart, summery fruit crumble under a raft of melting ice cream. In the words of Tina Fey's Liz Lemon, "I want to go to there."

Fruity desserts take beautifully to baking on a sheet pan and allow us to coax out the best flavor from gorgeously roasted plums, berries, apples, and more. In this chapter, you'll find recipes for simple but stunning baked fruit (like Slow-Roasted Tipsy Peaches, page 185), fruity meringue confections (like Orange & Cream Mini Pavlovas, page 171), and plenty of flaky pastry pairings (see Apple Pandowdy, page 191, or the Plum Pistachio Galette, page 179). And let's not forget about slab pie! The ultimate in fruit-to-crust ratios! When you need pie for a crowd, a slab pie is the way forward (see the Four-Striped Fruit Pie, page 174, for an option that should please all palates).

A few things to remember: When working with pie or galette dough, colder is better. If at any point the dough feels too soft and warm, just pop it in the refrigerator or freezer for a spell to chill—it will be easier to work with, for one, and will ultimately hold its shape better in the oven. When checking for doneness, in general, look for golden brown pastry and cheerfully bubbling fruit.

Cranberry Gingerbread Galette

SERVES 8 TO 10

Made with a gingerbread-spiced dough tucked around a bright, tart fresh cranberry filling, this galette is an unexpected way to bring classic holiday flavors to life, like a pie-shaped mash-up between gingerbread cookies and cranberry sauce, in the best possible way. Just be sure to serve the galette slightly warm, with big scoops of cool vanilla ice cream.

If you can't find fresh cranberries, fresh blueberries make a good substitute; just reduce the sugar in the filling by ½ cup.

Crust

- 1 cup (2 sticks) unsalted butter, at room temperature
- ½ cup granulated sugar
- 2 large eggs
- 2 teaspoons pure vanilla extract
- 3 cups all-purpose flour, plus more for dusting
- ¾ teaspoon kosher salt
- ½ teaspoon baking powder
- 2 teaspoons ground ginger
- 2 teaspoons ground cinnamon
- ½ teaspoon ground allspice
- ½ teaspoon ground cloves
- 1 teaspoon water
- Turbinado sugar

Filling

- 4 cups fresh cranberries (16 ounces)
- 1 cup granulated sugar
- ½ cup packed brown sugar
- 2 tablespoons all-purpose flour
- 2 tablespoons fresh orange zest
- ¼ cup fresh orange juice
- 1 teaspoon ground ginger
- ½ teaspoon ground cinnamon
- ¼ teaspoon kosher salt

- Vanilla ice cream, for serving (optional)

1. MAKE THE CRUST: In the bowl of a stand mixer fitted with the paddle attachment or in a large bowl with a handheld mixer, cream together the butter and granulated sugar on medium-high speed until fluffy and smooth, 3 to 5 minutes. Add 1 egg and the vanilla and beat until smooth, 1 minute more. Add the flour, salt, baking powder, ginger, cinnamon, allspice, and cloves and mix on low speed until the dough just comes together without any streaks. Gather the dough into a flat disc, wrap in plastic wrap, and refrigerate for at least 30 minutes, or up to 1 day.

2. When ready to bake, preheat the oven to 350°F with a rack in the center position. Line a sheet pan with parchment paper.

3. MAKE THE FILLING: In a large bowl, stir together the cranberries, granulated sugar, brown sugar, flour, orange zest, orange juice, ginger, cinnamon, and salt.

4. On a lightly floured surface, roll the gingerbread dough out into a large oval, about ¼ inch thick. Gently transfer the dough to the prepared pan.

5. Pour the cranberry filling into the center of the dough and spread it evenly with a rubber spatula, leaving a 1-inch border. Fold the edges of the dough over the filling, pinching any cracks together to seal.

6. In a small bowl, whisk the remaining egg with the water, then brush the egg wash over the galette crust. Sprinkle liberally with turbinado sugar. Bake the galette for 30 to 40 minutes, until the crust is deeply browned and the filling is gently bubbling. Allow the galette to cool for about 10 minutes.

7. Slice the galette into wedges and serve with a scoop of vanilla ice cream on top, if desired. The galette will keep, tightly covered, in the refrigerator for up to 4 days.

Orange & Cream Mini Pavlovas

SERVES 6

Basically an extra-elegant version of a large, crispy-edged marshmallow topped with whipped cream and fruit, individual pavlovas are always a dinner-party-dessert showstopper, but no one needs to know how simple they are to prepare! After whipping up the egg whites, the oven takes on most of the work, gently baking the fluffy meringues until their shells are crisp. Then all that's left to do is dollop on the whipped cream and slice up some juicy fruit. I love the sweet and tart combination of orange and cream in this simple yet stunning treat.

Meringues

4 large egg whites

Kosher salt

1¼ cups sugar

1 teaspoon cornstarch

2 teaspoons apple cider vinegar

2 teaspoons pure vanilla extract

Assembly

1½ cups heavy cream, cold

3 tablespoons sugar

½ cup orange marmalade

3 medium oranges, cut into suprêmes (see tip below)

1. Preheat the oven to 250°F with a rack in the center position. Line a sheet pan with parchment paper.

2. In the bowl of a stand mixer fitted with the whisk attachment or in a large bowl with a handheld mixer, whip the egg whites and a pinch of salt on medium-high speed until smooth, soft peaks form, about 3 minutes. With the mixer running, very slowly add the sugar, a tablespoon at a time. Once all of the sugar has been incorporated, increase the mixer speed to high and whip until the meringue forms stiff peaks, 3 to 5 minutes. Gently fold in the cornstarch, vinegar, and vanilla with a rubber spatula.

3. Scoop ½-cup mounds of the meringue onto the prepared pan (you should have six total). Shape them into rough circles and use the back of a spoon to swoop out a small divot in the center of each mound. Bake the mini pavlovas for 30 to 40 minutes, until they feel dry to the touch. Turn off the oven and let the meringues cool in the closed oven for at least 1 hour or up to overnight.

4. Just before serving, in the bowl of a stand mixer fitted with the whisk attachment or in a large bowl with a handheld mixer, whip the cream and sugar on medium-high speed until medium peaks form, about 5 minutes. Fold in the marmalade with a rubber spatula.

5. Scoop the marmalade cream over the pavlovas, dividing evenly. Top each pavlova with a few orange segments and serve immediately.

How do I: Suprême an orange?

Suprêming an orange (or any citrus fruit) is just fancy kitchen talk for "cut out the segments of orange flesh, leaving any skin or membrane behind." To do it, cut off both ends of the orange and stand it up on a cutting board on one of the cut sides. Use a paring knife to slice off the peel, starting from the top and following the curve of the fruit to the bottom. Repeat until all of the skin and pith (that tough white membrane) has been removed. Then, use the paring knife to gently slice the orange segments loose from between the tougher membranes, so you're left with clean, glistening slices of fresh citrus. You did it! You are a suprêmer supreme!

Big Peach Cobbler

SERVES 16 TO 20

The beauty of a cobbler lies in its sweet simplicity: juicy, baked fruit under a golden cap of lightly sweet, soft-but-crunchy-edged batter (a sort of biscuit-meets-pancake situation). It should be easy to throw together on a warm summer day and happily served for both dessert after dinner (under a scoop of ice cream, perhaps) and also for breakfast the next morning (this time with a spoonful of good yogurt on top). This big peach cobbler covers all the bases in terms of ease and simplicity—no blanching or peeling required—and the sweet batter comes together in minutes with just a bowl and a whisk. It's also quite adaptable, so if you'd like to use another kind of stone fruit instead of peaches, or if you get the urge to throw a handful of fresh berries or pitted cherries into the mix, feel free!

Unsalted butter or nonstick cooking spray

4 pounds fresh peaches (about 7 large), pitted and sliced

¼ cup packed brown sugar

Zest and juice of 1 lemon

2 tablespoons pure vanilla extract

2 teaspoons cornstarch

½ teaspoon plus a pinch of kosher salt

1½ cups all-purpose flour

¾ cup granulated sugar

1 tablespoon baking powder

½ teaspoon ground cinnamon

1 cup whole milk

½ cup (1 stick) unsalted butter, melted

½ teaspoon pure almond extract

Vanilla ice cream, for serving (optional)

1. Preheat the oven to 350°F with a rack in the center position. Grease a sheet pan with butter.

2. On the prepared pan, toss together the peaches, brown sugar, lemon zest and juice, 1 tablespoon of the vanilla, the cornstarch, and a pinch of salt until the peaches are well coated. Spread in an even layer.

3. In a large bowl, whisk together the flour, granulated sugar, baking powder, remaining ½ teaspoon salt, and the cinnamon. Add the milk, melted butter, remaining 1 tablespoon vanilla, and the almond extract and whisk gently just until smooth. Pour the batter over the peaches and spread as evenly as possible (there will be plenty of fruit peeking out from beneath the batter). Bake the cobbler until the topping is deeply golden and the filling is bubbling, about 30 minutes.

4. Scoop out portions and serve warm with scoops of ice cream, if you'd like. Leftover cobbler will keep, tightly wrapped, in the refrigerator for up to 5 days (rewarm it for 1 minute in the microwave before serving).

Four-Striped Fruit Pie

SERVES 24

This is one of the more involved recipes in this book, but it makes four pies in one! There's room on a sheet pan for everyone's favorite pie, so why not just make them all? One big crust and four simple fruit fillings later, you'll be able to please everyone at the table with this gorgeous striped pie. If you'd rather not fiddle with piecrust decorations, you can roll out the top crust, cut a few steam vents, and simply drape it over all four of the fillings, but I love the stripy, patchwork look of pairing a different crust with each filling, so if time allows, do have fun with it.

Crust

5 cups all-purpose flour, plus more for dusting

3 tablespoons granulated sugar

2½ teaspoons kosher salt

2 cups (4 sticks) unsalted butter, cut into cubes and chilled, plus more for greasing

1 cup ice-cold water

4 large graham crackers, crushed into crumbs

1 large egg

1 teaspoon water

Turbinado sugar

Fillings

3 cups fresh or frozen sweet cherries, pitted

¾ cup granulated sugar

8 tablespoons cornstarch

8 tablespoons fresh lemon juice (from about 3 lemons)

Kosher salt

4 cups thinly sliced peeled apples (from 2 to 3 apples; I like a mixture of Granny Smith, Golden Delicious, and Fuji)

1 teaspoon ground cinnamon

Zest of 1 orange

¼ cup packed brown sugar

3½ cups fresh blueberries

Zest of 2 lemons

3½ cups sliced peeled peaches (fresh or frozen)

½ teaspoon ground cardamom

1. MAKE THE CRUST: In a large bowl, whisk together the flour, granulated sugar, and salt. Add the butter and use your fingertips or a pastry cutter to work it into the dry ingredients, working quickly so it does not get too warm, until broken down to the size of small lentils and large pebbles. Add the cold water ½ cup at a time and work it in with your hands or a wooden spoon until the dough comes together.

2. Use your hands to gather the dough into a large, cohesive ball (if it's too dry and crumbly, add more water 1 tablespoon at a time until it really comes together, but do not overwork the dough—no kneading here). Divide the dough into two equal rectangular pieces and wrap each one tightly with plastic wrap. Refrigerate for about 1 hour, or up to 2 days.

3. MEANWHILE, MAKE THE FILLINGS: In a medium bowl, toss the cherries with ¼ cup of the granulated sugar, 2 tablespoons of the cornstarch, 2 tablespoons of the lemon juice, and a pinch of salt and mix gently to combine and coat the fruit thoroughly.

4. In a separate medium bowl, toss together the apples, cinnamon, orange zest, brown sugar, 2 tablespoons of the cornstarch, 2 tablespoons of the lemon juice, and a pinch of salt until the fruit is well coated.

5. In a third medium bowl, toss together the blueberries, half of the lemon zest, ¼ cup of the granulated sugar, 2 tablespoons of the cornstarch, 2 tablespoons of the lemon juice, and a pinch of salt until the berries are well coated.

6. In a fourth medium bowl, toss the peaches with the ground cardamom, remaining lemon zest, ¼ cup granulated sugar, 2 tablespoons cornstarch, 2 tablespoons lemon juice, and a pinch of salt.

7. When ready to bake, preheat the oven to 375°F with a rack in the center position. Grease a sheet pan with butter.

8. Generously flour a work surface and a rolling pin. Unwrap 1 piece of dough and roll it out to a 20 × 16-inch rectangle, working quickly so the dough doesn't get too warm and become difficult to work with (if it does, transfer the dough to a parchment-lined sheet pan and pop it back into the refrigerator or freezer for a few minutes to firm up).

9. Flour your hands and gently fold the dough in half like a book, then set it over the prepared pan with the folded edge over the center of the pan and carefully unfold. Gently press and lift the dough up and over the edges of the pan on all sides; there should be ½ inch of overhang all around. Sprinkle the graham cracker crumbs evenly over the bottom crust.

10. With a long side of the sheet pan nearest to you, pour the cherry mixture over the far left quarter of the crust, spreading into an even stripe. Spread the apple mixture next to the cherry mixture to fill another quarter; half the bottom crust should be covered at this point. Pour the blueberry mixture next to the apples over another quarter of the crust, then finish with the peach mixture to fill the pan. Some of the fruit and juices will mix together where the fillings meet. Refrigerate the pie while you prepare the top crust.

11. Roll out the second piece of dough on a generously floured surface to a 19 × 15-inch rectangle. Use a sharp knife to cut the dough crosswise into four thick strips, each about 3¾ inches wide. Cut each dough strip differently—you can cut out shapes, lattices, or decorative steam vents!

12. Lay each top crust design over one portion of the filling. Use kitchen shears to trim any dough that hangs over the edges of the pan by more than ½ inch. Gently pinch the top and bottom crusts together, folding and tucking the overhanging dough under itself around the edges of the pan to make a smooth border. Use your fingers or a fork to crimp the edges of the crust all the way around.

13. In a small bowl, whisk together the egg and water. Brush the top of the pie with the egg wash and sprinkle generously with turbinado sugar. Bake the pie for 50 to 60 minutes, rotating the pan halfway through, until the crust is deeply golden brown and the fillings are bubbling. Allow the pie to cool in the pan for about 20 minutes.

14. Slice the pie into pieces, either keeping the flavors separate or mixing them together, and serve warm or at room temperature. The pie will keep, tightly covered, in the refrigerator for 3 to 4 days.

photograph follows

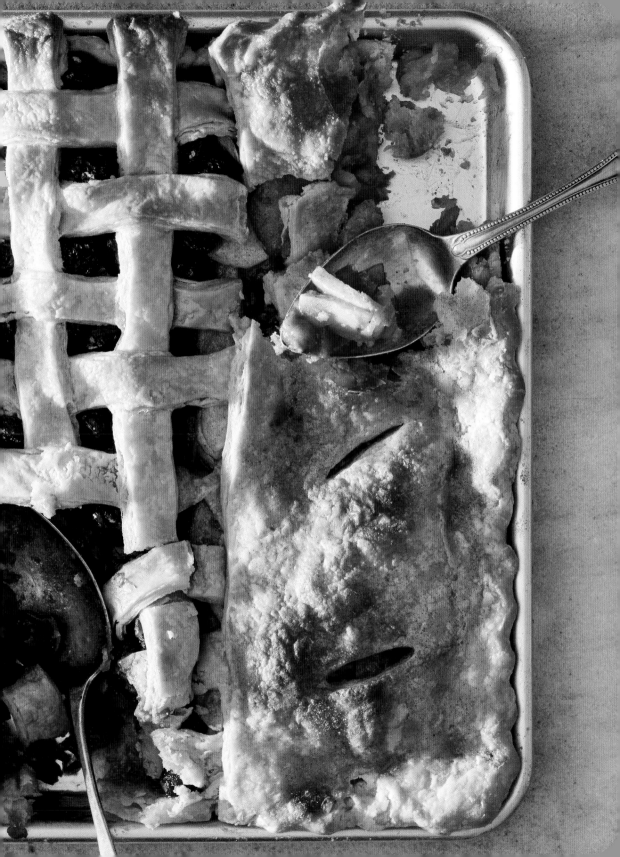

Plum Pistachio Galette

SERVES 6 TO 8

This bronzed free-form pie is one of the most elegant desserts in this book, and the most beautiful way to showcase ripe summer and fall fruit. Although with three home-made elements (piecrust, pistachio frangipane, and fruit filling), it may seem intimidating, I promise it's quite simple to pull together! And if you want to use store-bought piecrust instead of making your own, my lips are sealed. No shame, just a gorgeous galette ahead.

Crust

2 cups all-purpose flour, plus more for dusting

½ teaspoon kosher salt

1 tablespoon granulated sugar

¾ cup (1½ sticks) unsalted butter, cut into cubes and chilled

½ cup ice-cold water

Pistachio Frangipane

1 cup roasted, salted pistachios

⅓ cup unsalted butter, at room temperature

½ cup granulated sugar

Zest of 1 orange

1 large egg

½ teaspoon pure vanilla extract

Plums

5 small plums (about ¾ pound), pitted and sliced into thick wedges

Zest of ½ orange

1 tablespoon fresh orange juice

1 tablespoon granulated sugar

Assembly

1 large egg, beaten, or 1 tablespoon heavy cream

1 teaspoon turbinado sugar

Pistachio or vanilla ice cream, for serving

1. MAKE THE DOUGH: Add the flour, salt, and granulated sugar to a food processor. Pulse for about 5 seconds to combine. Add the butter and pulse about 10 times, until broken down into bits of various sizes. While pulsing, pour in the water and mix until the dough starts to come together, about 30 seconds.

2. Turn out the dough onto a lightly floured surface. Flour your hands and gather the dough into a flat disc; it will be a bit wet and sticky. Wrap tightly in plastic wrap and refrigerate until firm, at least 1 hour or up to 1 day. (Alternatively, chill in the freezer for about 30 minutes.)

3. Preheat the oven to 375°F with a rack in the center position. Line a sheet pan with parchment paper.

4. Generously flour a work surface and a rolling pin. Unwrap the dough, set it on the floured surface, and roll it out to a large circle about ¼ inch thick. Carefully transfer the dough to the prepared pan. Place the pan, uncovered, in the refrigerator or freezer to firm up the dough while you make the filling.

5. MAKE THE PISTACHIO FRANGIPANE: In a food processor, pulse the pistachios about 10 times, until coarsely ground. Remove 2 tablespoons of the ground pistachios and set aside for garnish. Add the butter, granulated sugar, orange zest, egg, and vanilla to the remaining pistachios in the food processor and pulse into a smooth paste, about 1 minute.

recipe continues

6. MAKE THE PLUMS: In a large bowl, toss the plums with the orange zest, orange juice, and granulated sugar until well coated.

7. ASSEMBLE THE GALETTE: Remove the dough from the refrigerator. Spread the pistachio paste evenly over the dough with a small offset spatula, leaving a 1-inch border. Arrange the plum wedges tightly atop the frangipane. Fold the dough over the plums, overlapping when necessary, to create a free-form crust. Brush the exposed crust with the beaten egg, then sprinkle with the turbinado sugar. Bake the galette about 30 minutes, until the crust is brown and the filling is bubbling.

8. Sprinkle the reserved ground pistachios on top of the galette. Slice into wedges and serve warm with generous scoops of pistachio ice cream. The galette can also be served at room temperature. It's best the day it's made, but will keep, tightly covered, in the refrigerator for 2 to 3 days.

Black & Blue Berry Slab Pie

with Basil Lime Sugar

SERVES 24

What's better than a giant home-made Pop-Tart? A giant homemade Pop-Tart sprinkled with basil lime sugar! This berry slab pie is exactly that—a double-crusted, purple-berry-filled pastry, baked to golden-brown perfection and topped with a sweet, tart, and herby green sugar. Thalia Ho includes a recipe for Basil Sugar Poundcakes in her book, Wild Sweetness, *and I found the idea of basil sugar to be positively brilliant. It's a beauti-ful topper to many desserts, but I especially love how it both comple-ments and enhances the flavors of the summer berries here.*

Crust

5 cups all-purpose flour

3 tablespoons sugar

2½ teaspoons kosher salt

2 cups (4 sticks) unsalted butter, cut into cubes and chilled

1 cup ice-cold water, plus more as needed

Berry Filling

5 heaping cups fresh blackberries

5 heaping cups fresh blueberries

Zest of 1 lemon

¼ cup fresh lemon juice (from about 1 lemon)

¾ cup sugar

6 tablespoons cornstarch

½ teaspoon kosher salt

Assembly

Unsalted butter or nonstick cooking spray

1 large egg

1 teaspoon water

Basil Lime Sugar

Zest of 1 lime

¼ cup packed fresh basil leaves

½ cup sugar

1. MAKE THE CRUST: In a large bowl, whisk together the flour, sugar, and salt. Add the butter and use your fingertips or a pastry cutter to work it into the dry ingredients, working quickly so it does not become too warm, until broken down to the size of small lentils and very large pebbles. Add the cold water ½ cup at a time and work it in with your hands or a wooden spoon until the dough comes together.

2. Use your hands to gather the dough into a large, cohesive ball (if it's too dry and crumbly, add more water 1 tablespoon at a time until it really comes together, but do not overwork the dough—no kneading here). Divide the dough into two equal rectangular pieces and wrap each tightly with plastic wrap. Refrigerate for at least 1 hour or up to 2 days.

3. MEANWHILE, MAKE THE BERRY FILLING: Add the blackberries and blueberries to a large bowl with the lemon zest, lemon juice, sugar, cornstarch, and salt. Toss gently to combine and coat the fruit thoroughly.

4. When ready to bake, preheat the oven to 375°F with a rack in the center position. Grease a sheet pan with butter.

5. Generously flour a work surface and a rolling pin. Unwrap one piece of dough and roll it out to a 20 × 15-inch rectangle, about ¼ inch thick, working quickly so the dough doesn't get too warm and become difficult to work with (if it does, transfer the dough to a parchment-lined sheet pan and pop it back into the refrigerator or the freezer for a few minutes to firm up).

recipe continues

6. Flour your hands and gently fold the dough in half like a book, then set it over the prepared pan with the folded edge over the center of the pan and carefully unfold. Gently press and lift the dough up and over the edges of the pan on all sides; there should be ½ inch of overhang all around.

7. Pour the berry mixture over the bottom crust, spreading it in an even layer with a rubber spatula. Transfer to the refrigerator while you roll out the top crust.

8. On a generously floured surface, roll out the remaining piece of dough to a 19 × 14-inch rectangle just over ¼ inch thick. Use a sharp knife to make a few thin slits (steam vents) in the top crust, then carefully drape over the filling. Use kitchen shears to trim any dough that hangs more than ½ inch over the edges of the pan. Gently pinch the top and bottom crusts together, folding and tucking the overhanging dough under itself around the edges of the pan to make a smooth border. Use your fingers or a fork to crimp the edges of the crust all the way around.

9. In a small bowl, whisk together the egg and water. Brush the egg wash over the top of the pie. Bake the pie for 50 to 60 minutes, rotating the pan halfway through, until the crust is deeply golden brown and the filling is bubbling.

10. MEANWHILE, MAKE THE BASIL LIME SUGAR: In a food processor or blender, pulse together the lime zest, basil, and sugar for about 20 seconds, until bright green, fine, and fragrant.

11. Sprinkle the green sugar generously over the still-warm pie. Cut the pie into pieces and serve warm or at room temperature. The pie will keep, tightly covered, in the refrigerator for 3 to 4 days.

Slow-Roasted Tipsy Peaches

SERVES 6 TO 8

Slow roasting any fruit is a surefire way to coax out its purest, very best flavor, and these peaches are no exception. Drizzle them with a buttery brown sugar mixture that will bubble and caramelize as it bakes, then serve the juicy, slumped fruit with a booze-laced whipped cream and a scattering of cookie crumbs for crunch. Nectarines, apricots, plums, or even pears will work here instead of peaches, though you may have to adjust the baking time (smaller fruit won't need as long in the oven). If you'd like to omit the booze, vanilla extract substitutes nicely.

4 large peaches, halved and pitted

4 tablespoons (½ stick) unsalted butter, melted

¼ cup packed plus 2 tablespoons brown sugar

¾ teaspoon ground cinnamon

1 tablespoon fresh lemon juice

2 tablespoons brandy, bourbon, or pure vanilla extract

1 cup plain full-fat Greek yogurt

1 cup heavy cream

1 whole vanilla bean, seeds scraped (see tip, page 126)

Large handful of crunchy cookies, such as amaretti, gingersnaps, or Biscoff, crumbled

1. Preheat the oven to 325°F with a rack in the center position. Line a sheet pan with parchment paper.

2. Arrange the peaches on the prepared pan, skin side down.

3. In a medium bowl, whisk together the melted butter, ¼ cup of the brown sugar, the cinnamon, lemon juice, and 1 tablespoon of the brandy. Pour the mixture evenly over the peaches. Bake the peaches until tender, but not losing their shape, about 40 minutes.

4. Meanwhile, in a large bowl, whisk together the yogurt, cream, vanilla bean seeds, the remaining 2 tablespoons brown sugar, and remaining 1 tablespoon brandy until thick and smooth.

5. Top the warm peaches with the whipped yogurt cream and sprinkle the cookie crumbs on top. Serve immediately. Leftover peaches will keep, tightly wrapped, in the refrigerator for up to 3 days.

How Do I: Pit a Peach?

The easiest way to pit a peach is to first make sure you're buying the proper variety of peach—specifically, freestone peaches. Freestone peaches are, happily, the variety of peach you're most likely to find at the grocery store, and unlike the other variety, called clingstone, freestone peaches will release their pits willingly, without the flesh clinging on for dear life (and making it very difficult to pull that pit!). Once you've got your freestone peaches, just use a paring knife to slice through the peach until you hit the pit. Then, run your knife all the way around the pit, twist the fruit into two halves, and gently pull the pit out. If you've gotten clingstones by mistake, don't fret—you'll just need to gently slide your paring knife under the top and bottom of the pit to release it from the fruit.

Eton's Largest Mess

SERVES 8 TO 10

Eton mess is a classic British dessert, usually a tumbled mix of broken meringue, cream, and fresh fruit layered together in a dainty glass. It's a beautiful combination of textures—the smooth cream a nice foil for the crunchy meringue and sweet fruit. Although the ingredients get all jumbled together, Eton mess somehow still manages to be both beautiful and posh. I thought it might be fun to get big and even more messy with it, and though you could certainly go with tradition and serve this in a fancy vessel, there's something fun and extra friendly about serving it right from the sheet pan.

4 large egg whites

Kosher salt

1¼ cups plus 3 tablespoons granulated sugar

1 teaspoon cornstarch

2 teaspoons apple cider vinegar

2 teaspoons pure vanilla extract

2 pounds fresh strawberries, stemmed and hulled

Zest and juice of 1 lime

¼ cup confectioners' sugar

1½ cups heavy cream, cold

1. Preheat the oven to 250°F with a rack in the center position. Line a sheet pan with parchment paper.

2. In the bowl of a stand mixer fitted with the whisk attachment or in a large bowl with a handheld mixer, whip the egg whites and a pinch of salt on medium-high speed until smooth, soft peaks form, about 3 minutes. With the mixer running, very slowly add 1¼ cups of the granulated sugar, a tablespoon at a time, then increase the mixer speed to high and whip until the meringue forms stiff peaks, 3 to 5 minutes. Gently fold in the cornstarch, vinegar, and vanilla with a rubber spatula to combine.

3. Use a ¼-cup measure to scoop mounds of the meringue onto the prepared pan (you should have 12 total), and shape into rough circles with a spoon or small offset spatula. Bake the meringues for 30 to 40 minutes, until they feel dry to the touch but haven't taken on much color. Turn off the oven and let the meringues cool in the closed oven for at least 1 hour or up to overnight.

4. Put half the strawberries in a large bowl and mash with a potato masher until broken down into a chunky puree. Thinly slice the remaining strawberries and add to the bowl, along with the lime zest and juice, confectioners' sugar, and a pinch of salt and toss gently to combine. Cover the bowl and let the strawberry mixture sit for at least 20 minutes at room temperature (or cover and chill in the refrigerator overnight).

5. Just before serving, in the bowl of a stand mixer fitted with the whisk attachment or in a large bowl with a handheld mixer, whip the cream with the remaining 3 tablespoons granulated sugar on medium speed until medium peaks form, about 5 minutes.

6. Remove half the meringues from the pan and set aside. Lightly crush and break up the remaining six meringues on the pan into large and small chunks, scattering in an even layer. Dollop the whipped cream in large scoops over the meringue shards, then top with generous spoonfuls of the macerated strawberries. Crumble the reserved meringues on top. Serve the enormous Eton mess in big scoops directly from the pan. Leftovers will keep, tightly wrapped, in the refrigerator for 1 day.

Sweet Cherry Shortcakes

SERVES 6 TO 8

When plump, sweet cherries are in season, I'm hard-pressed to do anything besides eat them fresh by the bowlful, but these simple short-cakes make a good case for pulling out the cherry pitter. The drop-biscuit-style dough is straight-forward to make and only faintly sweet, the perfect foil for freshly whipped cream and a tumble of macerated fresh cherries. If you can't find it in you to stem and pit a pound of fresh cherries, fresh peaches, strawberries, or raspber-ries would work nicely instead.

2 cups all-purpose flour

8 tablespoons granulated sugar

2 teaspoons baking powder

1 teaspoon kosher salt

⅔ cup buttermilk, cold

1 large egg

½ cup (1 stick) unsalted butter, melted and cooled

Turbinado sugar

2 pounds fresh cherries, stemmed and pitted

2 tablespoons cherry brandy, kirsch, or lemon juice

½ cup heavy cream, cold

1 teaspoon pure vanilla extract

1. Preheat the oven to 450°F with a rack in the center position. Line a sheet pan with parchment paper.

2. In a large bowl, whisk together the flour, 1 tablespoon of the granulated sugar, the baking powder, and salt.

3. In a large, spouted measuring cup or medium bowl, whisk together the buttermilk and egg until smooth. Add the melted butter and stir until small clumps form.

4. Pour the buttermilk mixture into the dry ingredients and stir with a rubber spatula until a shaggy dough comes together and no dry streaks remain.

5. Use a ⅓-cup measure to scoop the dough onto the prepared baking sheet, spacing about 2 inches apart. You should have 6 biscuits. Sprinkle each biscuit generously with turbinado sugar. Bake for about 15 minutes, until the tops of the biscuits are golden brown and crisp. Allow the biscuits to cool on the pan for 5 minutes, then transfer to a wire rack to cool completely.

6. Meanwhile, in a large bowl, toss the cherries with 6 table-spoons of the granulated sugar and the cherry brandy and gently mash with a fork or potato masher until some of the cherries are smashed and some are still whole. Let sit for 20 minutes.

7. In the bowl of a stand mixer fitted with the whisk attachment or in a large bowl with a handheld mixer, combine the cream, remaining 1 tablespoon granulated sugar, and the vanilla. Whip on medium-high speed until medium-soft peaks form, 3 to 5 minutes.

8. Split each biscuit in half, generously spoon some of the cherry mixture (and any juices) over the bottom biscuits, dollop a few tablespoons of whipped cream on top, and cap with the biscuit tops. Serve immediately.

9. Leftover biscuits (unassembled) will keep, tightly covered, at room temperature for 1 day. Rewarm in a 350°F oven for 3 to 5 minutes before topping with the cherries and cream and serving. The cherry mixture can be stored in an airtight container at room temperature for a few hours, or in the refrigerator overnight.

Simple Summer Fruit Crisp

SERVES 24

When summer fruit is at its finest and it's too hot to fuss in the kitchen, this simple crisp is the perfect way to manage dessert for a crowd. It's endlessly adaptable, as it will work with whatever fruit you have on hand, and comes together in minutes. It's also easy to make ahead and rewarm in a low oven before serving. So we'll get juicy, bubbling fruit and a golden, crispy topping, a perfect bed for a good scoop of ice cream, without toiling in a hot kitchen all day. Back to sipping chilled wine on the patio! Dessert (and next morning's breakfast, come to think of it) is handled.

I love the combination of stone fruit and berries here for a nice mix of color, texture, and flavor underneath the crisp topping. My favorite combinations include plums and cherries, peaches and blueberries, and apricots and fresh raspberries.

Unsalted butter or nonstick cooking spray

8 cups sliced stone fruit (such as peaches, nectarines, plums, and/or apricots)

2 cups fresh berries or pitted cherries

¾ cup granulated sugar

Zest and juice of 1 lemon

6 tablespoons cornstarch

1 teaspoon kosher salt

1½ cups all-purpose flour

1½ cups rolled oats

½ cup packed brown sugar

½ teaspoon ground cinnamon

½ cup (1 stick) unsalted butter, melted

1 teaspoon pure vanilla extract

Vanilla ice cream, for serving

1. Preheat the oven to 375°F with a rack in the center position. Grease a sheet pan with butter.

2. On the prepared pan, toss together the stone fruit, berries, granulated sugar, lemon zest and juice, cornstarch, and ½ teaspoon of the salt until the fruit is well coated, then spread in an even layer all the way to the corners.

3. In a large bowl, whisk together the flour, remaining ½ teaspoon salt, the oats, brown sugar, and cinnamon. Pour the melted butter and vanilla over the dry ingredients and stir with a rubber spatula until a clumpy dough comes together.

4. Scatter the crumble topping over the fruit by the handful, clumping it together in big and small chunks, until most of the fruit is covered. Bake the crisp for about 30 minutes, until the topping is browned and the fruit is bubbling around the edges. Allow the crisp to cool for 5 to 10 minutes in the pan.

5. Serve the crisp warm with scoops of ice cream on top. Leftover crisp will keep, tightly wrapped, in the refrigerator for up to 4 days.

Apple Pandowdy

SERVES 24

A classic American pie(ish), pandowdy consists of warm, sweet fruit under a baked crust. If you love a high fruit-to-crust ratio, pandowdy is your girl. Sure, there are some who may call her frumpy, but that's entirely by design—pressing the (store-bought! easy-peasy!) pastry crust down into the bubbling juices midway through baking results in a downright gorgeous flavor and crispy-soft texture.

Unsalted butter or nonstick cooking spray

8 to 10 apples (I like a mix of Granny Smith and Golden Delicious), peeled, cored, and sliced into ¼-inch-thick wedges

½ cup packed brown sugar

1 tablespoon ground cinnamon

1 teaspoon ground ginger

½ teaspoon ground nutmeg

½ cup crème fraîche

1 tablespoon pure vanilla extract

1 teaspoon kosher salt

⅓ cup all-purpose flour

Zest of 1 lemon

1 tablespoon fresh lemon juice

1 (17-ounce) package frozen puff pastry, thawed and sliced into 2-inch squares

1 large egg

1 teaspoon water

Turbinado sugar

Vanilla ice cream, for serving

1. Preheat the oven to 400°F with a rack in the center position. Grease a sheet pan with butter.

2. In a large bowl, toss the apples with the brown sugar, cinnamon, ginger, nutmeg, crème fraîche, vanilla, salt, flour, lemon zest, and lemon juice until well coated.

3. Pour the apple mixture onto the prepared pan and spread it evenly to the corners. Arrange the puff pastry squares on top of the apples, overlapping in places, until covered.

4. In a small bowl, beat the egg with the water, then brush the egg wash on top of the puff pastry pieces and sprinkle liberally with turbinado sugar. Bake for 30 minutes, then reduce the oven temperature to 350°F and use a spatula or large wooden spoon to gently press the puff pastry crust down into the warm fruit juices. Continue baking for another 30 minutes, until the crust is deeply browned and the filling is bubbling.

5. Serve the pandowdy warm with generous scoops of vanilla ice cream. Leftovers will keep, tightly wrapped in the refrigerator, for up to 4 days.

photograph follows

Fancy Fresh Fruit Tart

SERVES 6

Fresh fruit tarts are a staple in French bakeshop windows, their glistening fruit arranged just so, like gems in a jewel box, over crisp pastry beds lined with smooth vanilla custard. They always look so fancy and sophisticated, so it didn't cross my mind that you could easily make them at home until pastry school. At school, we made our own pâte brisée crust, whisked up vanilla pastry cream from scratch, and glazed our tarts with fresh apricot jam. We could certainly do the same at home, but a few shortcuts here and there (store-bought puff pastry, a clever pastry cream "cheat," and a simple dusting of confectioners' sugar to finish) simplify the process without sacrificing either flavor or elegance. Voilà—pâtisserie chez vous!

Crust

1 large egg

1 teaspoon water

All-purpose flour

1 sheet frozen puff pastry, thawed

1 tablespoon turbinado sugar

Filling

1½ cups heavy cream, cold

6 tablespoons boxed instant vanilla pudding mix

4 to 5 tablespoons whole milk

2 tablespoons orange liqueur, such as Grand Marnier

Topping

3 cups sliced fresh fruit (I like strawberries and kiwi)

Confectioners' sugar

1. Preheat the oven to 400°F with a rack in the center position. Line a sheet pan with parchment paper.

2. In a small bowl, whisk together the egg and water.

3. On a lightly floured surface, roll the puff pastry out to a 14 × 11-inch rectangle. Use a sharp knife to slice a ½-inch-wide strip from each long side of the pastry rectangle, then slice ½-inch-wide strips from each of the short sides. Brush the egg wash over the edges of the large pastry rectangle, then arrange the strips around the edges of the rectangle, forming a raised border all around. Brush the border and center of the pastry rectangle lightly with egg wash and sprinkle the turbinado sugar over just the border. Use a fork to prick the center of the pastry all over (this is called docking and will help steam escape and prevent the crust from puffing up too much in the oven). Bake the tart shell for 15 to 20 minutes, until deeply golden brown and puffed. Allow the shell to cool completely, about 25 minutes.

4. MAKE THE FILLING: In the bowl of a stand mixer fitted with the whisk attachment or in a large bowl with a handheld mixer, whip together the cream and pudding mix on medium speed until smooth and firm, about 3 minutes. Add the milk and orange liqueur and whisk until the pastry cream is smooth and spreadable.

5. Spread the pastry cream evenly over the center of the cooled tart shell and arrange the sliced fruit on top. Dust a bit of confectioners' sugar on top and serve immediately. The tart is best right after assembly, though you could bake the tart shell and prep the pastry cream 1 day in advance (store the tart shell loosely covered at room temperature and the pastry cream in an airtight container in the refrigerator).

Plum Dumplings

SERVES 8

Although the name sounds like something from a nursery rhyme (Little Boy Blue, Little Miss Muffet, Jack Horner . . . Plum Dumpling?), these beauties are in fact just sweet pockets of jammy fruit in a flaky pastry wrapper. Packed up with some butter and brown sugar, the fruit softens and caramelizes at the edges but keeps its integrity throughout, creating a beautiful mix of texture and sweet fruit flavor. If you can't get your hands on plums, these little packets also work nicely with large apricots or smaller nectarines.

½ cup (1 stick) unsalted butter, at room temperature

½ cup packed brown sugar

½ teaspoon ground cinnamon

½ teaspoon kosher salt

Zest of 1 lemon

All-purpose flour

2 sheets frozen puff pastry, thawed

4 medium plums, halved and pitted

1 large egg

1 teaspoon water

Turbinado sugar

Vanilla ice cream, for serving (optional)

1. Preheat the oven to 400°F with a rack in the center position. Line two sheet pans with parchment paper.

2. In a medium bowl, mash the butter, brown sugar, cinnamon, salt, and lemon zest into a smooth paste with a fork.

3. On a lightly floured surface, roll out 1 sheet of puff pastry to a 14-inch square. Use a sharp knife to cut the pastry sheet into four equal 7-inch squares. Repeat with the remaining sheet of puff pastry. Place the squares on the prepared pans, 4 per pan.

4. Scoop 1 tablespoon of the brown sugar–butter paste onto the lower left portion of each pastry square, then place a plum half, cut side down, on top.

5. In a small bowl, whisk together the egg and water.

6. Brush the egg wash over the edges of each puff pastry square. Fold the top right corner of each puff pastry square over the plum half, stretching the dough and pressing down at the seams to seal. Brush the corners of the triangles with a bit more egg wash and fold around the plums to form cute little packages. Poke the tines of a fork into the tops of each dumpling to create small air vents, then press the fork around the edges of the pastry to create a tight seal. Brush more egg wash on top of the dumplings and sprinkle liberally with turbinado sugar. Bake the dumplings until quite brown and puffed, about 20 minutes. Allow the dumplings to cool on the pan for 5 minutes.

7. Serve the plum dumplings warm, with a scoop of ice cream alongside, if desired.

Breakfast & Breads

Making Mornings Sweeter

Breakfast is by far my favorite meal of the day, so even though this is a book about sheet pan sweets, I had to include some good brunchy options for your morning table. In keeping with the title of this book, all of the recipes in this chapter are sweet, not savory (with the exception of the Focaccia, page 214— it's so wonderful and easy on a sheet pan that it had to be included), so you'll find lots of breakfast cakes and confections here instead of eggs and bacon. If you're like me, you hem and haw about what to order when out to brunch—eggs benedict or pancakes? Scramble or French toast? And you'll probably order the eggs, very sensibly, but then feel immediate buyer's remorse. Or maybe you'll order the eggs but get the pancakes "for the table," which honestly is a move that I deeply respect.

The recipes here are the sweet, indulgent, "for the table" kind, and I promise you won't regret a single one. Whether you need something cute and easy for the baby shower brunch (try the Blueberry Muffin Cake, page 209), want to impress the family on Christmas morning (Cinnamon Roll Poke Cake, page 216, for the win), or just need some breakfast cake to the face, stat (I'd go with the Dozen Donut Cake, page 213), the recipes in this chapter are designed to make the most delicious additions to your special morning meal.

Currant Lemon Cream Scones

MAKES 8 TO 10 SCONES

There's a wonderful bakery here in Seattle called Coyle's Bakeshop, and when my eldest son, Calder, was born, I made it part of my bleary-eyed new-mom routine to stop there midmornings for coffee and a treat. Once, when he was about nine months old, Calder became very interested in his mother's cream scone, and I vividly remember the first time he tried a bite, his big blue eyes wide with sugar and delight. After that first taste, baby Calder would polish off a full scone by himself every time we went to the bakery, which, as you may have guessed, was on the regular. These currant lemon cream scones will forever remind me of those blissful but exhausting days as a brand-new mom, and though I still visit the bakeshop frequently, I can make this recipe and be instantly transported back to the days when my biggest son was my tiny baby.

These scones can be flash-frozen before baking, then baked off right from frozen—just wait to brush them with cream until right before they go in the oven. If you can't find currants, which are tiny and sweet and lovely, you could sub in raisins or another dried fruit, finely chopped.

2¼ cups all-purpose flour, plus more for dusting

1 tablespoon baking powder

½ teaspoon baking soda

½ teaspoon kosher salt

¼ cup granulated sugar

Zest of 2 lemons

½ cup dried currants

½ cup (1 stick) unsalted butter, cut into cubes and chilled

½ cup heavy cream, cold, plus more for brushing

1 large egg

1 teaspoon pure vanilla extract

Turbinado sugar

1. Preheat the oven to 400°F with a rack in the center position. Line a sheet pan with parchment paper.

2. In a large bowl, whisk together the flour, baking powder, baking soda, salt, and granulated sugar. Add the lemon zest and dried currants and mix with a fork to thoroughly combine. With a pastry cutter (or your fingers), work the butter into the flour mixture, stopping when the butter pieces are well coated and roughly the size of lentils (or a bit larger).

3. In a small, spouted measuring cup or bowl, combine the cream, egg, and vanilla.

4. Pour the wet ingredients into the flour mixture and mix gently with the fork until just combined. The dough will look shaggy and a bit crumbly.

5. Transfer the dough to a lightly floured work surface and press into an 8 × 6-inch rectangle, roughly 1 inch thick. Use a sharp knife to cut the dough into 8 to 10 triangles. Place the triangles on the prepared baking sheet, spacing them evenly.

6. Brush the tops of the scones with cream and sprinkle generously with turbinado sugar. Bake the scones for about 10 minutes, until set and golden brown around the edges.

7. Serve the scones warm or at room temperature. The scones are best the day they're made, but will keep in an airtight container at room temperature for 2 to 3 days.

Apple Fritter Cake

SERVES 24

To me, the apple fritter is always the best choice at the donut shop. Every time. I mean, I'll never say no to a maple old-fashioned or a plain raised glazed, and there's a time and place for fancy shapes, fillings, and toppings, but if it's in the case, the apple fritter has my vote. You can't beat the dense yet airy dough, studded with pockets of apple and cinnamon and bathed in a milky glaze. This cake is an homage to my favorite donut—it's got the same dense crumb, baked apple pockets, and sweet maple glaze. And the best part? No frying necessary.

Cake

Unsalted butter or nonstick cooking spray

2½ cups all-purpose flour

½ teaspoon baking soda

1 teaspoon kosher salt

1 teaspoon ground cinnamon

¼ teaspoon ground nutmeg

2 cups packed dark brown sugar

½ cup (1 stick) unsalted butter, melted and cooled

1 cup canola oil

4 large eggs

1 teaspoon pure vanilla extract

1 teaspoon pure almond extract

4 cups chopped peeled apples (about 3 large; I like a mix of Granny Smith and Golden Delicious)

Glaze

4 tablespoons (½ stick) unsalted butter

¾ cup confectioners' sugar

2 tablespoons maple syrup

¼ teaspoon ground cinnamon

¼ teaspoon kosher salt

1 tablespoon whole milk

1. MAKE THE CAKE: Preheat the oven to 325°F with a rack in the center position. Grease a sheet pan with butter.

2. In a medium bowl, whisk together the flour, baking soda, salt, cinnamon, and nutmeg.

3. In a large bowl, whisk together the brown sugar, melted butter, and oil until smooth. Add the eggs, vanilla, and almond extract and whisk well to combine.

4. Add the dry ingredients to the wet ingredients and stir with a rubber spatula until the dough just comes together. Fold in the apples until evenly distributed.

5. Pour the batter into the prepared pan and spread it evenly to the corners with a large offset spatula. Bake for 20 to 25 minutes, until the cake is deeply golden and the edges just start to pull away from the sides of the pan. Set the sheet pan on a wire rack and let the cake cool for 20 to 25 minutes.

6. MAKE THE GLAZE: Melt the butter in a small pot over medium heat. Cook, stirring often with a rubber spatula, until the butter turns a toasted, amber color (it will bubble and spit; when it quiets down, check for browning). Whisk in the confectioners' sugar, maple syrup, cinnamon, salt, and milk until smooth.

7. Drizzle the glaze evenly over the cooled cake. Let set for 5 minutes.

8. Slice the cake into pieces and serve. The cake is best the day it's made, but will keep, tightly covered, in the refrigerator for 3 to 4 days.

Cinnamon Nut Wreath

SERVES ABOUT 10

Fun fact: The state of Wisconsin has an official state pastry called a kringle, a wreath-shaped flaky Danish pastry with a tender, buttery crust and sweet filling. Do more states have official representative pastries? Why not?! Someone should do something about this.

In the meantime, here's my (very streamlined) version of the kringle—a braided puff pastry wreath stuffed with a sweet, nutty filling and drizzled with a buttery vanilla glaze. It's a real stunner on the brunch table for the holidays and is highly snackable as the day wears on. If you're hosting a house full of relatives, beware—you might see little slivers disappearing here and there, a subtle licking of fingers, and then, like magic, the whole thing's vanished.

Pastry Wreath

- 7 ounces almond paste
- ½ cup chopped walnuts
- ½ cup chopped pecans
- 1 tablespoon ground cinnamon
- ½ cup (1 stick) unsalted butter, at room temperature
- ½ cup packed brown sugar
- ½ teaspoon kosher salt
- 2 large eggs
- All-purpose flour
- 2 sheets frozen puff pastry, thawed
- 1 teaspoon water
- Turbinado sugar

Glaze

- 1 cup confectioners' sugar
- 2 tablespoons unsalted butter, at room temperature
- 1 teaspoon pure vanilla extract
- 2 tablespoons whole milk or heavy cream

1. MAKE THE PASTRY WREATH: Preheat the oven to 400°F with a rack in the center position.

2. Add the almond paste, walnuts, pecans, cinnamon, butter, brown sugar, salt, and 1 of the eggs to a food processor. Pulse for 1 minute, until combined into a thick, chunky paste.

3. Set a large piece of parchment paper on a work surface and lightly flour the parchment and a rolling pin. Roll out both sheets of puff pastry to 10 × 15-inch rectangles, about ¼ inch thick.

4. In a small bowl, whisk together the remaining egg and water.

5. Set the puff pastry sheets next to each other with the short sides touching. Brush the short side of one of the sheets with egg wash, then gently press the short side of the other one on top, overlapping the sheets by about ¾ inch, to create one long, rectangular piece of dough with a long side of the rectangle nearest to you.

6. Use a sharp knife to cut off the top left and bottom left corners of the rectangle at a 45-degree angle away from the left side of the pastry, leaving a 4-inch-long edge of dough between them. Next, move to the top right and bottom right corners and cut out two triangular notches, again leaving a 4-inch-long edge of dough along the right side of the pastry between (the whole thing will look like a sideways, short-stumped Christmas tree missing its pointy top). Finally, make diagonal slits, about 1 inch apart and parallel to the notches, along the top and bottom of the pastry, leaving a 4-inch-wide strip in the center intact. (The narrow flaps will get folded over to make the braid, with the filling in the center.)

7. Spread the nutty filling over the center strip of pastry (not on the side flaps), leaving a ¾-inch border at the left and right edges.

recipe continues

8. Fold the left and right edges of the pastry over the filling. Then, starting from the left side and alternating top and bottom flaps, fold the diagonal flaps of pastry tightly over the filling, crisscrossing them on top of one another, until all of the strips are interwoven and the filling is completely covered. Trim away any loose pieces of pastry, then bring the ends of the braid together to form a wreath and pinch the seams to seal.

9. Carefully transfer the parchment with the wreath to a sheet pan. Lightly brush the top and sides of the braid with the egg wash and sprinkle with turbinado sugar. Bake the wreath until the pastry is deeply browned, 30 to 40 minutes. Allow to cool on the pan for about 20 minutes.

10. MEANWHILE, MAKE THE GLAZE: In a medium bowl, whisk together the confectioners' sugar, butter, vanilla, and milk until smooth.

11. Drizzle the glaze generously over the wreath. Slice into thin wedges and serve. The wreath is best the day it's made, although it can be baked ahead and stored, unglazed and tightly covered, at room temperature for 1 day. Reheat it in a 350°F oven for 10 to 15 minutes, until crisp, then glaze before serving. Any leftovers will keep, tightly covered, at room temperature for up to 3 days.

Blueberry Muffin Cake

SERVES 20 TO 24

Why scoop and bake two dozen individual muffins when you can bake a whole blueberry muffin cake, complete with a tender crumb topping, on a single sheet pan? (No good reason, that's why.) This blueberry muffin cake has it all—a moist, vanilla-flavored base with hints of lemon, bright pops of fresh blueberries, and, yes, that superb crumb top. Slice it into cute squares and pile it high on a platter for brunch. I promise you won't miss the muffins.

Unsalted butter or nonstick cooking spray

Crumb Topping

½ cup (1 stick) unsalted butter, melted

⅓ cup granulated sugar

⅓ cup packed brown sugar

1¼ cups all-purpose flour

1 teaspoon ground cinnamon

¼ teaspoon kosher salt

Cake

2¼ cups all-purpose flour

1 tablespoon baking powder

¾ teaspoon baking soda

1 teaspoon kosher salt

¼ teaspoon ground nutmeg

¾ cup (1½ sticks) unsalted butter, at room temperature

1¼ cups granulated sugar

Zest of 1 lemon

4 large eggs

1½ cups sour cream

1 tablespoon pure vanilla extract

2 cups fresh blueberries, plus more for topping

Turbinado sugar

1. Preheat the oven to 350°F with a rack in the center position. Grease a sheet pan with butter.

2. MAKE THE CRUMB TOPPING: In a medium bowl, whisk together the melted butter, granulated sugar, and brown sugar until well combined. Add the flour, cinnamon, and salt and stir with a wooden spoon until a thick dough forms.

3. MAKE THE CAKE: In a medium bowl whisk together the flour, baking powder, baking soda, salt, and nutmeg.

4. In the bowl of a stand mixer fitted with the paddle attachment or in a large bowl with a handheld mixer, cream together the butter, granulated sugar, and lemon zest on high speed until light and fluffy, about 3 minutes. Beat in the eggs one at a time on medium-high speed, scraping down the sides of the bowl after each addition until fully incorporated (the mixture may look curdled, but will smooth out as you add the rest of the ingredients). Add half the dry ingredients and mix on low speed to incorporate, then mix in the sour cream and vanilla. Add the remaining dry ingredients and beat on low speed until just a few streaks remain. Fold in the blueberries with a rubber spatula.

5. Pour the batter onto the prepared pan and spread it evenly to the corners with a large offset spatula. Break up the crumb topping into uneven clumps with your fingers and scatter over the batter, all the way to the edges of the pan. Tuck a few blueberries into some crumb topping crevices, if you'd like, and sprinkle the top with a bit of turbinado sugar. Bake for 15 to 20 minutes, until a tester inserted into the center comes out clean. Set the sheet pan on a wire rack and let the cake cool in the pan for at least 15 minutes.

6. Slice the cake into pieces and serve. The cake will keep, tightly covered, in the refrigerator for up to 4 days.

photograph follows

Dozen Donut Cake

SERVES 24

As a child (and, fine, probably also as an adult), there was nothing more exciting to me than when my grandpa would come to visit and set a whole box of donuts on the kitchen counter upon arrival. The apple fritter was for him—no touching Gramps's fritter—but the rest were for my sisters, cousins, aunts, and uncles to snack on as we pleased. To me, it was like Santa Claus himself had stopped by with a sack full of presents, and I loved inspecting that box of donuts, full of sandy sugar and colorful glazes, then carefully making my selection. This dozen donut cake is a fun way to re-create the magic of an assorted box in sheet cake form. It's buttery and soft, full of warm nutmeg flavor, and can be sugared and glazed and sprinkled however you like to create your favorite combinations.

Cake

Unsalted butter

6 large eggs, at room temperature

2½ cups granulated sugar

½ cup (1 stick) unsalted butter, melted and cooled

1 cup canola oil

2 cups buttermilk

1 tablespoon pure vanilla extract

4 cups all-purpose flour

1 tablespoon ground nutmeg

1 tablespoon baking powder

1 teaspoon baking soda

1 teaspoon kosher salt

Glazes and Topping

1 cup confectioners' sugar

2 tablespoons whole milk, plus more as needed

½ teaspoon pure vanilla extract

2 tablespoons unsweetened cocoa powder

¼ cup granulated sugar

¼ cup ground cinnamon

4 tablespoons (½ stick) unsalted butter, melted and cooled

¼ cup sprinkles

1. MAKE THE CAKE: Preheat the oven to 350°F with a rack in the center position. Grease a sheet pan with butter.

2. In a large bowl, vigorously whisk together the eggs and granulated sugar for 1 minute, until well combined and very frothy. Whisk in the melted butter, oil, buttermilk, and vanilla until smooth.

3. Add the flour, nutmeg, baking powder, baking soda, and salt and gently fold with the whisk until the batter is smooth and streak-free.

4. Pour the batter into the prepared pan and spread it evenly to the corners with a large offset spatula. Bake for 18 to 20 minutes, until the cake is golden, pulls away from the sides of the pan, and a tester inserted into the center comes out clean. Run a paring knife around the edges of the cake to loosen, and then let it cool in the pan for 15 minutes.

5. MEANWHILE, MAKE THE GLAZES: In a medium bowl, whisk together ¾ cup of the confectioners' sugar, the whole milk, and vanilla until smooth and pourable, like donut glaze. Scoop half the glaze into a small bowl and whisk in the cocoa powder and more milk until the same consistency as the vanilla glaze is reached.

6. In a small bowl, whisk together the granulated sugar and cinnamon until well combined.

7. Brush the melted butter all over the cake, then sift thick stripes of the remaining ¼ cup confectioners' sugar and the cinnamon sugar (be generous) and spread thick stripes of the vanilla and chocolate glazes on top. Decorate with sprinkles.

8. Slice the cake into pieces, either keeping the flavors separate or mixing them together. The cake will keep, tightly covered, at room temperature for up to 3 days (you may want to sift more confectioners' and cinnamon sugar on top before serving if the cake absorbs the original dusting after sitting).

Simple Focaccia

SERVES ABOUT 24

Ever since I watched the "Fat" episode of Samin Nosrat's delightful Netflix series Salt, Fat, Acid, Heat, *I've wanted to move to Italy and submerge myself in an olive-oil-slicked pan of focaccia dough, with giant, yeasty air bubbles fighting toward the surface, fat flakes of sea salt raining down from overhead. I haven't made it to Italy yet, but it turns out that good focaccia is fun and easy to make at home, so I figure I'm halfway there. Once baked, the bronzed crust of this homemade focaccia gives way to a soft, bouncy interior, and while it's perfect as is, it takes well to additional toppings; I've given you a few of my favorite options.*

Focaccia

- 5 cups all-purpose flour
- 1 tablespoon kosher salt
- 1 teaspoon sugar
- 2 cups lukewarm water
- 1 (¼-ounce) packet instant yeast (2¼ teaspoons)
- 7 tablespoons extra-virgin olive oil, plus more for greasing
- Flaky sea salt, such as Maldon

Suggested Topping Combinations

- 1 tablespoon each minced garlic and fresh rosemary
- 1 tablespoon za'atar and ½ cup halved cherry tomatoes
- 1 tablespoon chopped fresh thyme and the zest of 1 lemon

1. MAKE THE FOCACCIA: In a large bowl, whisk together the flour, kosher salt, and sugar.

2. In a large, spouted measuring cup, mix together the water, yeast, and 3 tablespoons of the olive oil.

3. Pour the wet ingredients into the dry ingredients and mix with a rubber spatula or wooden spoon until a shaggy dough comes together. Use your hands to knead the dough in the bowl (it will be a bit sticky) until it smooths out a bit.

4. Transfer the dough to a clean large bowl greased with olive oil and cover with plastic wrap. Allow the dough to rise overnight (or up to 48 hours) in the refrigerator.

5. Remove the bowl from the refrigerator and let the dough come to room temperature, about 1 hour.

6. Generously coat a sheet pan with the remaining 4 tablespoons olive oil. Turn out the dough onto the prepared pan, and gently press and stretch it (try to get it all the way to the corners, but don't stress out if it won't stretch completely—the dough will relax and spread out as it rises again). Let the dough sit at room temperature for an hour or two, uncovered, until it's puffed up and you can see large bubbles forming.

7. Preheat the oven to 425°F with a rack in the center position.

8. Using oiled hands, gently press your fingertips into the dough to dimple all over. Sprinkle flaky sea salt and any desired topping combination(s) over the dough.

9. Bake the focaccia for 15 to 20 minutes, until deeply golden brown and fragrant. Allow the focaccia to cool in the pan for 10 minutes.

10. Slice the focaccia and serve warm. The focaccia is best the day it's made, but will keep, tightly covered, at room temperature for up to 4 days. Warming it in the oven or toaster before eating is highly recommended.

Cinnamon Roll Poke Cake

SERVES 24

This fluffy white cake, poked and filled with cinnamon roll filling and slathered generously with cream cheese frosting, is the new way to cinnamon roll. No fussing with yeast, rolling out dough, or trying to make perfectly round slices with dental floss—let's just poke holes in a cake and be done with it.

If you'd like to make this ahead, feel free—the cake keeps very well overnight in the refrigerator. I highly recommend warming up slices for a few seconds in the microwave before serving, for that fresh, warm-from-the-oven cinnamon roll experience.

Cake

- 1 cup (2 sticks) unsalted butter, at room temperature, plus more for greasing
- 1¾ cups granulated sugar
- 3 large eggs
- 3 large egg whites
- 3 cups all-purpose flour
- 2½ teaspoons baking powder
- ½ teaspoon kosher salt
- 1¼ cups whole milk
- 1 tablespoon pure vanilla extract
- ¼ cup vegetable oil

Cinnamon Filling

- ¾ cup (1½ sticks) unsalted butter, melted
- ¾ cup packed brown sugar
- ¾ cup sweetened condensed milk
- 2 tablespoons ground cinnamon
- 1 tablespoon pure vanilla extract

Frosting

- 1 (8-ounce) package cream cheese, at room temperature
- ½ cup (1 stick) unsalted butter, at room temperature
- 2½ cups confectioners' sugar
- 3 tablespoons sweetened condensed milk
- 1 teaspoon pure vanilla extract

1. MAKE THE CAKE: Preheat the oven to 350°F with a rack in the center position. Grease a sheet pan with butter.

2. In the bowl of a stand mixer fitted with the paddle attachment or in a large bowl with a handheld mixer, cream together the butter and granulated sugar on medium-high speed until fluffy and light, 3 to 5 minutes. Add the eggs and egg whites one at a time, mixing well and scraping down the sides of the bowl after each addition, until combined.

3. In a medium bowl, whisk together the flour, baking powder, and salt.

4. In a large, spouted measuring cup, whisk together the whole milk, vanilla, and oil.

5. Add half the flour mixture to the butter mixture, beating on low speed just to incorporate. Add the milk mixture, continuing to beat until combined, then add the rest of the flour mixture and beat just until the batter comes together without any streaks.

6. Pour the batter into the prepared pan and spread it evenly to the corners with a large offset spatula. Bake for 20 to 24 minutes, until the cake bounces back when lightly poked and a tester inserted into the center comes out clean.

7. MEANWHILE, MAKE THE CINNAMON FILLING: In a medium bowl, whisk together the melted butter, brown sugar, condensed milk, cinnamon, and vanilla until smooth.

8. Remove the cake from the oven and, while it is still warm, use the handle of a wooden spoon (or a similar tool roughly ½ inch in diameter) to poke large holes in the cake about every inch or so, pressing almost, but not quite, through to the bottom. Immediately pour the cinnamon filling over the warm cake, working slowly and filling all of the holes. Allow the cake to cool completely, about 25 minutes.

9. MEANWHILE, MAKE THE FROSTING: In the bowl of a stand mixer fitted with the paddle attachment or in a large bowl with a handheld mixer, beat together the cream cheese and butter on medium-high speed until smooth, 3 to 5 minutes. Add the confectioners' sugar, condensed milk, and vanilla and beat until soft and smooth, another 2 to 3 minutes.

10. Spread the frosting evenly over the cooled cake, then slice into pieces and serve. The cake will keep, tightly covered, in the refrigerator for 3 to 4 days.

photograph follows

Sheet Pan Pancakes

SERVES 6 TO 8

This recipe is for when you want platefuls of pancakes without standing over the stove, carefully pouring batter and flipping each one individually. A sheet pan full of pancake batter also ensures that everyone is served hot pancakes at the same time, and no one (including the cook) is left waiting for that last batch to finish. These have the same fluffiness, crispy edges, and customizable topping options, but in a much more efficient package. Sheet pan pancakes for everyone!

Pancakes

10 tablespoons (1¼ sticks) unsalted butter

3 cups all-purpose flour

¼ cup granulated sugar

Zest of 1 lemon

1 tablespoon baking powder

1 teaspoon baking soda

1 teaspoon kosher salt

1½ cups buttermilk

1½ cups whole milk

1 teaspoon pure vanilla extract

2 large eggs

Topping and Serving

Fresh blueberries

Mini chocolate chips

Chopped bananas

Toasted shredded or flaked coconut

Chopped fresh strawberries

Unsalted butter

Maple syrup

Confectioners' sugar

1. Preheat the oven to 400°F with a rack in the center position.

2. Place the butter on a sheet pan and put the pan in the oven for 3 to 5 minutes, until the butter is melted and just starting to brown.

3. Meanwhile, in a large bowl, whisk together the flour, granulated sugar, lemon zest, baking powder, baking soda, and salt.

4. In a medium bowl or spouted measuring cup, whisk together the buttermilk, whole milk, and vanilla.

5. Remove the sheet pan from the oven and tilt it so the butter coats the pan evenly. Then, pour the hot butter into the cold milk mixture, whisking to combine. Whisk in the eggs.

6. Pour the wet ingredients into the dry ingredients and mix gently until a slightly lumpy batter comes together.

7. Pour the batter into the still-hot pan (if the pan has become cold, warm it for a few minutes in the oven first) and top with your desired toppings, either scattering them evenly all over the pan or creating separate sections for each one. Bake the pancakes for 12 to 15 minutes, until golden brown and pulling away from the edges of the pan. Allow the pancakes to cool for 3 minutes.

8. Slice the pancakes into large pieces and serve hot, with butter and maple syrup or a dusting of confectioners' sugar, if you'd like. Leftover pancakes can be flash-frozen and stored in an airtight container in the freezer for up to 2 months. Rewarm in the microwave for 30 to 60 seconds.

Pumpkin-Spiced Granola

MAKES 6 TO 8 CUPS

The pumpkin-spice-ification of just about everything has gotten a bit out of hand, I'll admit. But there are some things that undoubtedly benefit from the addition of pumpkin and spice—toothpaste? Hard no. Granola? Big yes!

Homemade granola is so easy and satisfying and I'm convinced that truly nothing makes a house smell better. Why buy luxury candles when you can pop a sheet pan of pumpkin-spiced granola in the oven? I mean, one will give you a headache and a giant dent in your wallet, and the other will net you an alluring signature scent and a delicious breakfast. A jar of homemade granola makes a lovely gift, so it may even win you a few friends to boot.

3 cups rolled oats

¾ cup wheat bran

¼ cup chia seeds

¼ cup flax seeds

1 cup pecans

¾ cup slivered almonds

1 cup unsweetened coconut flakes

½ cup hulled raw pumpkin seeds

2 tablespoons sesame seeds

1 cup canned pure pumpkin puree

¼ cup pure maple syrup

¼ cup extra-virgin olive oil

½ teaspoon kosher salt

½ teaspoon ground cinnamon

½ teaspoon ground ginger

¼ teaspoon ground cloves

¼ teaspoon ground nutmeg

A large handful of raisins, dried cranberries, and/or chopped dried apricots (optional)

1. Preheat the oven to 325°F with a rack in the center position.

2. Spread the oats, wheat bran, chia seeds, flax seeds, pecans, almonds, coconut, pumpkin seeds, and sesame seeds evenly over an unlined sheet pan, tossing gently to combine.

3. In a medium bowl, whisk together the pumpkin puree, maple syrup, olive oil, salt, cinnamon, cloves, and nutmeg until smooth.

4. Drizzle the pumpkin mixture over the dry oat mixture, then use your hands (or two spoons) to mix everything together until the granola mixture is damp and well coated. Spread the mixture evenly on the pan. Bake the granola for 30 to 45 minutes, stirring occasionally, until dry, very toasted, and quite fragrant. Allow the granola to cool completely on the pan, about 25 minutes. Stir in the dried fruit with a rubber spatula, if using.

5. Store the granola in airtight jars or zip-top bags at room temperature for up to 1 week, or in the freezer for up to 6 months.

Banana Buckwheat Coffee Crumb Cake

SERVES 20 TO 24

A tender crumb swirled through with brown sugar and espresso and topped with dark chunks of buckwheat crumble, this cake is a charming mash-up of banana bread and coffee cake. It's complex in flavor, both sweet from the banana and deep from the buckwheat and espresso, and brings a welcome change from the typical coffee cake experience. I particularly love the dark color and nutty, hoppy flavor that buckwheat flour brings to the crumb top, but if you don't have it on hand or just prefer to replace it with all-purpose flour, you certainly can.

Unsalted butter or nonstick cooking spray

Crumb Topping

⅔ cup granulated sugar

⅔ cup packed brown sugar

1 teaspoon ground cinnamon

½ teaspoon kosher salt

1 cup all-purpose flour

1½ cups buckwheat flour

1 cup (2 sticks) unsalted butter, melted

Coffee Swirl

½ cup packed brown sugar

1 tablespoon instant espresso powder

2 teaspoons ground cinnamon

Cake

1 cup granulated sugar

4 large eggs

2 cups mashed banana (from about 4 medium bananas)

1 cup sour cream

1 tablespoon pure vanilla extract

1 teaspoon kosher salt

3 cups all-purpose flour

1 tablespoon baking powder

¾ teaspoon baking soda

¾ cup (1½ sticks) unsalted butter, melted

1. Preheat the oven to 350°F with a rack in the center position. Grease a sheet pan with butter.

2. MAKE THE CRUMB TOPPING: In a medium bowl, whisk together the granulated sugar, brown sugar, cinnamon, salt, all-purpose flour, and buckwheat flour until well combined. Pour in the melted butter and stir with a wooden spoon or rubber spatula to bring together a thick dough.

3. MAKE THE COFFEE SWIRL: In a small bowl, whisk together the brown sugar, espresso powder, and cinnamon until combined.

4. MAKE THE CAKE: In a large bowl, vigorously whisk the granulated sugar and eggs together until pale and foamy, about 1 minute. Add the banana, sour cream, vanilla, and salt and whisk to combine. Add the flour, baking powder, and baking soda and stir until a thick batter comes together. Fold in the melted butter with a rubber spatula until smooth.

5. Pour half the batter into the prepared pan and spread it evenly to the corners with a large offset spatula. Sprinkle the coffee swirl evenly over the cake batter, then dollop the remaining cake batter on top of the coffee layer and gently spread it with the offset spatula until the coffee layer is covered completely. Break up the crumb topping unevenly with your fingers and scatter over the batter, all the way to the edges. Bake for 15 to 20 minutes, until a tester inserted into the center comes out clean. Let the cake cool in the pan for at least 15 minutes.

6. Slice the coffee cake into pieces and serve. The cake will keep, tightly covered, in the refrigerator for up to 4 days.

Orange Olive Oil Challah

with Raisins

SERVES 6 TO 8

If there's one lesson we all took away from months and months stuck at home, it's the joy of freshly baked bread. This beautifully bronzed challah, richly scented with olive oil and orange zest, is a doable project that yields striking results. Instant yeast and a simple three-strand braid take any intimidation out of pulling this loaf together, and a double egg wash, a neat little trick from iconic cookbook author Joan Nathan, ensures the most divinely burnished crust. If raisins aren't your thing, just leave them out, but don't skip the sprinkle of flaky sea salt before baking.

1 (¼-ounce) packet instant yeast (2¼ teaspoons)

¾ cup lukewarm water

¼ cup honey

⅓ cup olive oil, plus more for greasing

3 large eggs

1 teaspoon orange zest

4 cups all-purpose flour, plus more for dusting

2 teaspoons kosher salt

½ cup golden raisins

1 teaspoon cold water

Flaky sea salt, such as Maldon

1. In a large bowl, whisk together the yeast, lukewarm water, and honey until well combined and frothy. Whisk in the olive oil, 2 of the eggs, and the orange zest until well combined. Add the flour, kosher salt, and raisins and mix with a rubber spatula until a shaggy dough comes together.

2. Turn the dough out onto a lightly floured work surface and knead for 5 to 10 minutes, continuing to sprinkle the work surface and your hands with flour when necessary, until the dough is stretchy and smooth. Shape the dough into a ball and place it into a large bowl greased with olive oil.

3. Cover the bowl with plastic wrap and let it sit at room temperature for about 1 hour, until roughly doubled in size (alternatively, let the dough slowly rise in the refrigerator overnight; just let it come to room temperature for 60 to 90 minutes before moving on to the next step).

4. Turn out the dough onto a lightly floured work surface and divide it into three equal pieces. Use your hands to squeeze and roll each piece of dough into a long rope with tapered ends, measuring roughly 20 inches long and 1 inch wide. Pinch the ends of the ropes together and gently braid the strands, then coil the braid into a round loaf, tucking the loose end underneath.

5. Line a sheet pan with parchment paper, then transfer the challah to the pan.

6. In a small bowl, whisk together the remaining egg and the cold water. Brush the egg wash over the challah, then let the dough rise for another hour or so at room temperature, until puffed and pillowy.

7. About 15 minutes before baking, preheat the oven to 350°F with a rack in the center position.

8. Brush the challah again with the egg wash, then sprinkle lightly with flaky sea salt. Bake the challah for 45 to 60 minutes, until the crust is deeply burnished (if it gets too dark too quickly, tent a piece of aluminum foil over the challah—I usually do this about 25 minutes into cooking) and a thermometer inserted into the center reads 190°F. Let the challah cool on the pan for 10 minutes, then transfer to a wire rack to cool completely, about 1 hour.

9. The challah is best the day it's made, but will keep, tightly covered, at room temperature for up to 4 days (leftovers are wonderful toasted and slathered with butter).

recipe continues

Tell Me: **Can I Substitute Active Dry Yeast for Instant Yeast?**

Sold on store shelves in small packets or larger jars, both active dry yeast and instant yeast (sometimes called *rapid rise* or *quick rise* yeast) will help us leaven our bakes, and the short answer to whether or not they're interchangeable is a hearty YES! Technically, active dry yeast should be dissolved in some water before using, while instant yeast can be mixed right into the dry ingredients. But I've found that both work nicely when mixed right in, particularly in this challah recipe—the active dry yeast may just take an extra 15 to 20 minutes of rising time. Whichever kind you use, be sure to store your yeast in the refrigerator to keep it fresh and active.

Berry Bread Pudding

SERVES 15 TO 20

I love hosting brunch, but it's a lot of work to pull together a fabulous menu, beautifully set table, clean kitchen, clean children, and cute outfit all before ten a.m., so a make-ahead brunch dish is key. This berry bread pudding fits the bill—it's sweet, eggy, pretty with pops of bright fruit, and easily assembled the night before, so all you have to do is slide the pan into the oven in the morning. You may (unfortunately) even have time to change out of your pj pants.

Unsalted butter or nonstick cooking spray

1 large loaf of country bread (about 1½ pounds), sliced

2 cups mixed berries (I like sliced strawberries, raspberries, and blueberries)

5 cups whole milk

5 large eggs

3 tablespoons pure maple syrup, plus more for serving

1 teaspoon kosher salt

1 tablespoon pure vanilla extract

¼ cup mixed berry jam

Zest of 1 lemon

Turbinado sugar

Confectioners' sugar

1. Preheat the oven to 375°F with a rack in the center position. Grease a sheet pan with butter.

2. Cut the bread slices into thick strips, about 1 inch wide, and arrange evenly on the prepared pan. Scatter the mixed berries over and around the bread.

3. In a medium bowl, whisk together the milk, eggs, maple syrup, salt, vanilla, jam, and lemon zest.

4. Pour the custard mixture over the bread and fruit, then gently toss everything together so that all of the bread is coated. Spread everything evenly in the pan, then let the bread pudding sit for 5 minutes (or cover and refrigerate overnight) before sprinkling generously with turbinado sugar. Bake the bread pudding for 30 to 35 minutes, until well browned around the edges.

5. Serve the pudding scooped warm from the oven, with more maple syrup or a dusting of confectioners' sugar. Leftovers will keep, tightly wrapped, in the refrigerator for up to 4 days.

Raspberry Almond Bostock

SERVES 6 TO 8

A classic (though less well-known) French pastry, somewhere between French toast and an almond croissant, the bostock was invented as a delicious way to use up stale bread. (And yes, I agree, the name sounds like it belongs less in a French pâtisserie and more on an American football team roster . . . wide receiver, fullback, bostock.) No matter what we call it, this pastry's elegant face and flavor—crisp on the outside, soft and custardy within—belie its utter simplicity to make at home. Soak thick slices of brioche in a maple syrup mixture, spread on some good jam and almond cream, then cap it all off with sliced almonds and a mess of confectioners' sugar. It's an unexpectedly luxurious brunch to serve guests, or keep for yourself as a (well-deserved) weekend breakfast treat.

¼ cup pure maple syrup

⅓ cup boiling water

2 tablespoons rum, kirsch, amaretto liqueur, or pure vanilla extract

1 loaf of brioche (about 1 pound), sliced 1 inch thick

½ cup raspberry jam

1 cup roasted, unsalted almonds

½ cup (1 stick) unsalted butter, at room temperature

½ cup granulated sugar

½ teaspoon kosher salt

Zest of 1 orange

1 large egg

½ teaspoon pure vanilla extract

1 cup sliced almonds

Confectioners' sugar

1. Preheat the oven to 400°F with a rack in the center position. Line two sheet pans with parchment paper.

2. In a small bowl, whisk together the maple syrup, boiling water, and rum until combined.

3. Arrange the brioche on the prepared pans and brush each slice generously with the maple syrup mixture to soak through. Spread the raspberry jam evenly over each slice of bread.

4. In a food processor, pulse the roasted almonds 10 to 15 times, until coarsely ground. Add the butter, granulated sugar, salt, orange zest, egg, and vanilla and pulse into a smooth paste, 1 to 2 minutes.

5. Spread the almond frangipane evenly over the jam on the brioche slices, then top each slice with a sprinkle of sliced almonds. Bake the bostock for 8 to 12 minutes, until well browned and slightly puffed.

6. Dust each bostock generously with confectioners' sugar and serve warm. The bostock are best the day they're made, but will keep, tightly covered, in the refrigerator for up to 3 days. Toast the bostock in a 300°F oven to warm through before serving.

Index

Note: Page references in *italics* indicate photographs.

Acknowledgments

Writing a baking book takes a lot of butter, sweat, and tears—and lots of help to boot. I'm so thankful to the many people who made it possible for me to get this book out into the world! Endless thanks . . .

To you! For picking up this book, and maybe even baking from it. Thanks for trusting me with your dessert.

To Alyssa Reuben, agent extraordinaire. Thanks for keeping me on the level.

To my editor Amanda Englander and the entire team at Union Square & Co.—Caroline, Danielle, Jennifer, Melissa, Raphael, Lindsay, Kevin—for your steady guidance, moxie, and taste. Thanks for turning my half-baked ideas into a fully baked cookbook.

To my brilliant photography team, Dana Gallagher, Frances Boswell, and Pam Morris—you made this book beautiful.

To Maggie Gilbert, not only the very best aunt, but also the best recipe tester, tweaker, and brainstormer du monde. This whole thing just doesn't work without you.

To my trusted group of tasters and testers, including Sarah Barthelow, Emily Gilbert, Emily Horowitz, Casey Gilbert, Veronica Penney, the Moore family, and the entire Rosenbaum clan—thank you for baking and eating along with me.

To the amazing teachers at New Discovery School, for putting up with my carousel of Tupperware treats at drop-off, but mostly for keeping my boys in such kind and wonderful hands.

To the Friendship Friends, for being the best hype gals/group texters I could ever ask for.

To my entire family, both near and far, for the encouragement, love, and support (not to mention free childcare). Special thanks to Dots, Boo, Nana, and Poppi: I couldn't have done it without you.

To Ben, Calder, Jack, and Sadie, for the sweetest hugs and very honest feedback. Thanks for holding me up and doing the dishes. The Jeffreys to my Ina. I love you guys the most.

About the Author

Molly Gilbert, a graduate of Amherst College and the French Culinary Institute, is the author of *Sheet Pan Suppers* and *One Pan & Done*. She has worked as a recipe tester in the kitchen of *Saveur*, a cooking instructor, and a private chef, and she formerly ran the blog *Dunk and Crumble*. Her work has been featured on QVC, the *Today Show*, in the *Washington Post*, *Fine Cooking*, *Parade*, *Every Day with Rachael Ray*, and *The Kitchn*, among others. Molly is known for her simple yet elegant meals and desserts using fresh ingredients and streamlined techniques. Originally from the Philadelphia area, she currently lives in Seattle with her cookie-loving family.